CONNECTING
WITH
GOD

CONNECTING WITH GOD

14 Ways Churches Can Help People Grow Spiritually

Herb Miller

Abingdon Press
Nashville

CONNECTING WITH GOD:
14 WAYS CHURCHES CAN HELP PEOPLE GROW SPIRITUALLY

Library of Congress Cataloging-in-Publication Data

Miller, Herb.
    Connecting with God : 14 ways churches can help people grow spiritually/Herb
Miller.
    p. cm.
    Includes bibliographical references.
    ISBN 0-687-09405-4 (alk. paper)
    1. Mission of the church.   2. Spiritual formation.   3. Spiritual life—Christianity.
I. Title.
BV601.8.M55   1994
253—dc20   94-6697

94 95 96 97 98 99 00 01 02 03—10 9 8 7 6 5 4 3 2 1

MANUFACTURED IN THE UNITED STATES OF AMERICA

To Pearl Miller, the mother
who helped to plant seeds for this harvest

And to Olene Harlin, the mother-in-law
whose daughter nourished them with
spiritual encouragement

CONTENTS

Chapter 1

GROPING FOR
THE GOOD LIFE

"It's a good question," the woman said.

"What?" her husband asked, peering over his *Wall Street Journal.*

"We got this mail-order catalogue today. Look at all these exotic specialty items—they have everything, from authentic Russian KGB medals to handmade cigars from the Dominican Republic. They call it *The Good Life Catalog.*[1] I wonder, what does it take to have a 'good life'?"

"I'm not sure," he answered, his eyes moving back to the article on overseas marketing, "but you probably can't buy it through the mail."

Everyone, in some fashion, eventually asks that basic question: What does it take to have a good life? Usually, people ask it several times across the pages of their years. Something has changed, however, as the last few decades have unrolled into American culture. The present generation answers that question in a way somewhat different from the way their parents and grandparents answered it. Increasing percentages of people suspect that the spiritual dimension of life is a major factor in finding the answer. Evidence of this new interest in spirituality can be seen in the following examples.

- A *Time* news item says that "vacationers who have grown weary of white-water kayaking, dangling from cliffs and other trendy adventure trips are now turning to spiritual vacations featuring meditation and silence."[2]

- During a recent year, New Agers spent more than $100 million on quartz crystals believed to possess healing and thought-transmission powers. That same year, Americans spent another $300 million on audiotapes and books that promise spiritual self-fulfillment of every kind, including, in one case, "out of body experiences in thirty days."[3]

- An ABC documentary about the spiritual revival taking place in this country, titled "Search for Spirituality," focused on the varied ways Americans are trying to find God. It featured a gathering of five thousand Presbyterian women in Iowa and "creation-centered" rituals in California.[4] The follow-up program, called "Journey of the Heart," received a record number of viewer calls, requesting that the topic of spirituality be pursued in future programming.[5]

George H. Gallup, Jr., says that American people are eagerly and impulsively groping for ways to mature in their faith. Eight Americans in ten wish their faith were stronger. Three persons in four would like to see religious beliefs play a greater role in people's lives. Christians name spiritual growth a top priority more often than evangelism, supporting community causes, strengthening the local church, or influencing legislation.[6]

WHY NOW?

This spiritual quest did not seem as prominent during the middle decades of the 1900s. Why, then, is it appearing now? For several reasons, among which the following are significant.

- We tried drugs, but for most people, the trips did not live up to their billing. Speed and other such substances turned out to be fast roads to disaster. One Baby Boomer said that a pill someone put in his mouth gave him "the vision and courage to actually go after what I had been longing for my whole life, and that was a spiritual quest."[7] But few Americans still agree with that answer. Too many years of evidence have stacked up. The good life requires more than something you put in your mouth or your nose.

- The philosophy of "rational positivism" argued that science and education, given time, could provide the good life. That conviction, quite popular during the mid-1900s, seems far less appealing now. Church historian Martin Marty indicates that the picture for secular humanism—the popular name for rational positivism—is now clouded in the United States.[8]
- The pursuit of pleasure looked good to the survivors of World War II. We have now had plenty of experience with the new set of Ten Commandments: "1. Have a good day. 2. Shop. 3. Eliminate pain. 4. Be up-to-date. 5. Relax. 6. Express yourself. 7. Have a happy family. 8. Be entertaining. 9. Be entertained. 10. Buy entertainment."[9] They improve life, but not enough.

During a period of the French Revolution called the Reign of Terror, revolutionists killed even their friends. A French nobleman who had befriended the poor should have had no reason for concern. Yet he was forced into hiding. After the revolution, someone asked him what he did during the Reign of Terror. He replied grimly, "I stayed alive."

Many people find it difficult to stay alive these days. They have sorted through many good-life options. More years of education make them better informed. Aerobics and better eating habits make them physically more healthy. Yet people still grope for something better, something spiritual. Researchers tell us that the majority of them are confused about where to find it.[10]

COMPETING DEFINITIONS

People who discuss spirituality are not always talking about the same thing. Your viewpoint regarding the definition of spirituality depends on your point of view. Shirley MacLaine types, for example, seem to define spiritual maturity in terms far broader than the classic Christian view. For New Agers, spirituality relates to "human potential, ultimate progress, well-being, higher entities, wholeness, or openness to the infinite." This view tends to deemphasize, redefine, or totally abandon the classic, centuries-old concept of God, and urges us to look within ourselves to find transcendent powers.[11]

Christians, however, usually work from a more biblical perspective. They tend to build their definitions of spiritual maturity on foundations similar to those of the apostle Paul: "Have the mind of Christ" (I Cor. 2:16); "Let the same mind be in you that was in Christ Jesus" (Phil. 2:5). Thus, for Christians, spirituality concerns the movements of God's Spirit in personal life, in churches, and in the cosmos. In order to define the difference between religious education (the imparting of knowledge) and actually adopting the mind of Christ, a new term—spiritual formation—has appeared: "Spiritual formation is the dynamic process whereby the Word of God is applied by the Spirit of God to the heart and mind of the child of God, so that she or he becomes more like the Son of God."[12]

Many of the benefits of Christian spirituality are similar to those proposed by New Agers: a sense of peace derived from greater ability to handle frustration, a feeling of fulfillment, a sense of direction, self-confidence, and self-esteem. However, people who strive for Christian spiritual growth operate from a different worldview. Christian spirituality involves a positive relationship with God, with other human beings, and with God's creation. This kind of spirituality includes, but also transcends, all areas of one's being, generating meaning and purpose to life experiences.[13]

LIVING DEFINITIONS OF
CHRISTIAN SPIRITUALITY

Some of the most dependable research regarding spiritual maturity, from the classic Christian perspective, is reported by

George Gallup, Jr., and Timothy Jones in *The Saints Among Us.*[14] Gallup researchers have known for several years that 13 percent of Americans are highly committed to their religious faith. These 24 million of the 182 million adult Americans are the backbone of their communities and churches. Gallup and Jones built on this previous data with further polls among these "hidden saints." Gallup says that these people have a "transforming faith," a term most people would say is synonymous with spirituality, spiritual maturity, or optimum spiritual growth.[15] The behavior of persons in this group differs from the other 87 percent of Americans. Among the behaviors and beliefs these unusual personalities share, the following are especially obvious:

- They are much more likely to have a daily time of private prayer.
- They feel a genuine sense of the presence of God in their lives.
- They report that their religious experiences are a source of strength, personal growth, and healing of inner conflicts.
- They tend to have a greater sense of inner peace, to feel more joyful and happy, and are less likely to feel depressed.
- They are more humble and less likely to exhibit an inflated sense of self-importance.
- They are far more often engaged in compassionate acts for others.
- They are less racially prejudiced.
- They are far more capable of forgiving people who wrong them and of being constructive, reconciling members of society.
- They are more favorable toward church involvement in political activity in order to right wrongs in society.

This research contributes magnificently to our increasing understanding that Christian spirituality is a quality different from morality and ethics, with its roots other than in upbringing and genetics.[16]

LIMITED-EDITION PRINTS

From the classic Christian perspective, spiritual growth is the process of forming Christ in a human being. The Academy for Spiritual Formation, sponsored by The Upper Room in Nashville, Tennessee, has adopted Maxie Dunnam's definition of spiritual formation: "The dynamic process of receiving by faith and appropriating by commitment, discipline, and action, the living Christ into our lives to the end that our lives will conform to and manifest the living Christ in the world."[17] (To obtain Upper Room materials, see the Resources section.)

The good life does not equal "happiness," that tempting but blind-alley American preoccupation. Rather, the good life involves being remade in the image of Jesus. This kind of good life brings success of an order higher than happiness. Through becoming "conformed to the image of his Son" (Rom. 8:29), people discover the will of God for their lives and live in the middle of it. That is why Paul says that spiritual growth is of unlimited value, compared to physical growth (I Tim. 4:7-8). Moving toward the objective of Christ living in us (Gal. 2:20) produces the best good life of all.

A four-inch rain that fell in one hour resulted in a flash flood. The torrent flattened every tree on the valley floor, except one, which had grown on top of a gigantic boulder. Its roots were wrapped around that huge rock on their way into the soil. Likewise, spiritual growth for the Christian is never a movement toward some inner ideal that we self-select. Spiritual growth means building our lives around the Rock of Ages. This foundation is much more than a philosophy of living or a purposeful principle; it is a person—Jesus Christ.[18]

For Christians, maximum spiritual maturity means that they become as much like Christ as their humanity allows. They cannot become Christ, any more than the copy of a Michelangelo painting can become the original. But Christians can become limited-edition prints, if they let the image of the Master seep into the canvas of their days and experiences.

New Age philosophies seem to say that you should center in on yourself to find your highest meaning. Christian spirituality says the opposite—if you want the good life, connect yourself to the best life. A *Time* magazine article quotes an advertising executive who says that Baby Boomers exhibit a free-floating sense of searching for a value system. Their instincts seem to tell them, " 'Slow down. Figure out what's important.' But they haven't arrived at what that is."[19] Persons who connect with Christ have found it. They understand that spiritual maturity is not something you do. It is the direction in which you are headed because of the destination you have chosen.

The branch does not need to get up every morning and say to itself, "I must work hard, or there will be no grapes." The branch's power comes from staying connected to the vine. In the same way, God gives us spiritual growth as a gift, through the power of the Holy Spirit, as we connect and stay connected with Christ. "I am the vine, you are the branches . . . bear much fruit" (John 15:5).

When Paul says, "It is no longer I who live, but it is Christ who lives in me" (Gal. 2:20), he means that his personality has been reorganized around a new center. Instead of revolving around his ego, it centers on the Christ within. That is the target toward which the arrow of spiritual growth is headed. People who choose that direction engage in a lifetime process: They attempt to reorganize the main reference point of their personalities in ways that keep the ambitions and goals of their ego from being at the center. They cannot, of course, totally remove the ego. Even the most advanced of spiritual surgery does not achieve that. But they can delimit the ego's power as the controlling filter for all their thinking, feeling, and acting.[20]

GOD'S IRRIGATION SYSTEM

Various kinds of irrigation systems power the lush California agricultural valleys. The most basic of these is a simple gravity-flow process. Water from a ditch runs into the fields. Spiritual growth in human personality is like an irrigation system that waters a field containing three crops: (1) a loving, caring, positive relationship with other people; (2) a high level of commitment to God's goals of making the world a better, healthier, more caring place; and (3) significant levels of personal joy, peace, and satisfaction in daily living.

Our communication with God (talking to and listening to God) irrigates these three crops. This does not mean that our God communication is the *only* source of nurture for those three crops. The three positive qualities mentioned above— loving people, commitment to great causes, and life satisfaction—are nourished in other ways. Positive family environments and genetic codes can strengthen those positive qualities. But the research evidence indicates that these three crops grow largest in personality fields powered by spiritual communication with God. That is why Jesus urged people to "strive first for the kingdom of God" (Matt. 6:33). That is where the living-water power is.

Just as water flows to a level at all points in a container, the hydraulics of spiritual maturity has no dams, valves, or sluice gates. The water either flows into all three crops of our lives at the same time, benefiting each equally, or it flows into none of them. People cannot, for example, successfully seek personal satisfaction as the sole objective of spiritual growth. When one crop is watered, all three crops are watered equally. Refusing spiritual water for better relationships with people, or for the life-commitment crop, also retards the growth of personal satisfaction. All get water, or none get water.

This is what the writers of a new curriculum (developed in and for a Baby Boomer church that attracts 15,000 people each weekend) mean when they say that a disciple is one who walks with God, lives the Word, contributes to the work, and impacts the world.[21] In God's irrigation system, all the crops grow, or none grow. When they all grow, the good life happens.

Nor can spirituality stand alone—as a fascinating intellectual or emotional pursuit—unconnected to the soil of daily life. Spirituality that grows no visible crop is not spirituality, just as irrigation is not irrigation unless it irrigates something. Spirituality lives out the values derived from our God connection in personal human existence. That is why James says that faith without works is dead (James 2:26). An irrigation ditch with no outlets to crops becomes a stagnant pond. Spiritual growth is the whole person, related to God by the power of the Spirit of Jesus, the Christ. Unless that God connection has concrete results in daily life, it is not the kind of spirituality recommended by Jesus. The quality of your life mirrors your spiritual maturity, and vice versa. Low spiritual maturity—low life quality; high spiritual maturity—high life quality.

THE ULTIMATE BRAIN TRANSPLANT

Fetal-tissue transplants are showing dramatic results in medical researchers' pioneering efforts to treat Parkinson's disease. The *New England Journal of Medicine* reported on three studies that involved more than one hundred patients worldwide. Parkinson's sufferers who had trouble performing the most ordinary tasks slowly became able to walk without falling, assume more care of themselves, and even drive a car.[22] For these sufferers, the old joke about brain transplants has become a joyful reality.

Increasing numbers of people believe that they need something even more dramatic than a brain transplant; they need a soul transplant. As they search for the good life, at the very essence of their being—the spiritual dimension—they need major surgery.

African American leader Louis Sullivan illustrated the awesome power of spiritual reality when he reported watching a morning news show. Interviewing four former drug addicts, the host asked each one how he or she got off drugs.

The first replied, "Well, first I found Jesus. Jesus helped me to get off drugs."

This obviously threw the host, who had not intended to discuss religion. He hurried on to the second person: "What was it in your life that helped you get off drugs?"

"I started to church, and then I found Jesus," the second answered.

After getting a similar response from the third interviewee, the host said to the fourth, "Now, I'm sure you've had some kind of religious experience, but what else helped you to get off drugs?"

Louis Sullivan concluded his story this way: "Many are guilty of the same error—underestimating the influence and impact of spiritual solutions for the problems facing our Black community."[23]

Fewer and fewer people of every race make those kinds of underestimations regarding spirituality. Many people, from every racial and ethnic background—most of whom have less obvious and dramatic problems than a drug habit—yearn for the good life. They instinctively know that this is not just an educational or a psychological quest; it is a spiritual quest.

For many of those seekers, that dream becomes a reality. They cannot purchase this "pearl of great value" (Matt. 13:46) through a catalogue, but they discover that it is available.

Chapter 2

TENDING
TO BUSINESS

In 1836, London University constructed a new headquarters. Called the Senate House, it was the tallest building in London. Little was known about architecture at that time. Many people feared tall buildings. So the English government passed a law against occupying the top ten floors of the building, lest the whole thing fall down from the weight of the furniture and occupants. To this day, the top ten stories of the London University headquarters are unoccupied.

The most important elements of congregational life occur on the "top floors"—where people connect with God and experience spiritual growth. Yet, several scientifically conducted opinion polls indicate that Americans think most churches are failing at this, their most important role. The top floors appear largely unoccupied.

Young adults are especially likely to express that opinion. One-third of Americans born between 1946 and 1964 have dropped out of the church in which they grew up. Research by church sociologist William McKinney indicates that many of those under age forty-five who drop out of oldline Protestant congregations say they are looking for greater spiritual growth opportunities.[1] Another sociologist, Wade Clark Roof, notes that some of these Boomers are returning to church, but on different terms. Most of them "believe that religion is a spiritual quest, not a social obligation to churches and synagogues." Many say that they are not "religious," but "spiritual." For them, *religious* means institutional and conformist, while *spiritual* means personal and introspective: "Boomers are likely to say they are on a spiritual quest in search of faith."[2]

Evidence increasingly indicates that insufficient emphasis on evangelism may not be the only cause of membership decline in many denominations since 1965. Neglecting an emphasis on the primary reason people attend church—to connect with God and grow in that relationship—may be an equally important cause of membership decline. Sociologists David A. Roozen and C. Kirk Hadaway seem to support that thesis when they note that "denominational loyalty is out and congregational vitality is in." They say that the reason for that trend runs deeper than a mere 1960s-type rebellion from tradition. Many young adults see doctrinal positions as irrelevant. "People are not as interested in beliefs as they are in a personal relationship with or experience of the transcendent."[3]

That data is supported by research in growing congregations. Their leaders "place a greater emphasis on prayer, and most appear to make the spiritual growth of their members a major priority." Among churches that have moved off their membership growth plateau, 63 percent are rated by their pastors as excellent or good in the spiritual growth of their members—compared to only 34 percent of churches that continue on a numerical plateau.[4] Another study shows that churches characterized by a greater emphasis on spiritual development in their adult-education program also tend to be growing numerically.[5]

Despite the research evidence, however, many churches appear not to be tending to their primary business. At break time, during a workshop in Portland, Oregon, people lined up at a coffee urn. A big sign across it—apparently designed for in-house communication to church members—said, "Works great! Has all its parts!" For many Americans, the last half of that sign accurately describes their church. It has all its parts, but they no longer work together to produce spiritual growth.

USE IT OR LOSE IT

A marketing expert points out that churches play a unique role in society. They are the only social institutions designed to provide people with spiritual and moral nourishment: "It is the unique mission of religious organizations to raise our sights above the mundane tasks of 'getting and spending' to address the larger questions of personal purpose, service to others, what it means to be a fulfilled human being, and the mysteries of the cosmos."[6]

Churches accomplish their unique role by enriching, expending, and expanding: (a) They *enrich* the lives of members with spiritual growth, psychological nurture, and a sense of belonging; (b) They *expend* energy and resources to help needy people in the church, community, and world; (c) They *expand* by helping to touch people outside the church walls with the life-changing power of Jesus, the Christ. But *enrich* is the basic verb. Churches that do not spiritually enrich cannot *expand,* and they will *expend* less and less energy and resources to help the needy.

In 1909, the Associated Marketing Clubs of America met at the Galt House in Louisville, Kentucky, for their fifth annual convention. Led by Samuel C. Dobbs, they took action to challenge false advertising with a "truth in marketing" statement. This became a key concept in the launching of the Better Business Bureau. Truth in advertising has not been applied to congregations. It should be. When churches fail to live up to their central mission of helping people grow spiritually, they are engaged in false advertising, and the public quickly catches on.

In the final pages of the Church universal's operating manual, Paul recommends a focus for leaders that seems to fit the 1990s: "I pray that out of his glorious riches he may strengthen you with power through his Spirit in your inner being, so that Christ may dwell in your hearts through faith . . . that you may be filled to the measure of all the fullness of God" (Eph. 3:16-17, 19 NIV). In churches, this either happens, or does not happen. When it happens, people grow spiritually, and churches tend to grow numerically—not because they advertise effectively, but because they meet the basic need of the people who attend church. When this need is not met, no amount of advertising saves congregations from decline.

HOW DOES SPIRITUAL GROWTH HAPPEN?

Spiritual growth is obviously the basic reason churches open their doors. It is "the undertone, the tone, and the overtone of the Bible. It was the focus of the early church. It has been the impassioned concern of the saints of all ages."[7] A three-year study in six denominations concluded that the primary aim of congregations is to nurture a life-changing faith that will shape one's way of (a) thinking, (b) being, and (c) acting.[8]

But how, exactly, does spiritual growth happen? What can leaders of congregations do to facilitate it? When Peter, in his Pentecost sermon, urges people to make a spiritual connection to Christ, he quotes the Old Testament prophet Joel: "I will pour out my Spirit on all people" (Acts 2:17*b* NIV). We know that is possible. All of us have met people who are spiritually mature. How, exactly, does that come about? Is it a gift that God gives to only a few? If spiritual maturity can be taught or caught, how does that happen?

Church leaders who want to strengthen the spiritual-growth facilitating power of their congregations must recognize two seemingly opposite truths:

1. *Spiritual growth is a gift of God; it is not the self-manufactured quality that many New Agers seem to think.* (Nor is it a program that church bureaucrats can print and distribute.) A skilled

technician can repair an electric toaster, but the appliance must have electricity in order to function. In the same way, people do not grow spiritually, except through the touch of God.

2. *On the other hand, people do not become God-like without trying.* Trying is always a factor—as is deciding to live in an environment where trying is encouraged. Rick Warren says that spiritual growth is what happens when Christ is "resident and president of your life."[9] That election does not occur by write-in ballots. The seed of spiritual maturity either grows through watering or lies dormant through neglect.

Spiritual growth often begins, however, from a point outside the realm of personal volition or congregational engineering. For example, many people report that their initial spiritual growth resulted from a time of stress, an illness, a change in life circumstances, or the arrival of children. Their congregation played no role whatever. The touch of God began through a life experience. As one person said, "Spiritual growth began when I was broken and had only God to depend on." Sometimes, however, the touch of God comes in ways that seem totally unconnected with life's circumstances. Some people say, "I don't know why. I guess it was just my time."

A congregation's effectiveness in helping people connect with God and grow in that relationship is determined by a complex mixture of factors which fall into one of *two major categories:* (1) what God does by his Spirit's interaction within the flow of each individual's life, circumstances, and needs; and (2) what the congregation does to help meet the spiritual, psychological, emotional, and relational needs of individuals.

Initiating the development of spiritual maturity is primarily an act of God's Spirit. "The wind blows wherever it pleases," Jesus said. "You hear its sound, but you cannot tell where it comes from or where it is going. So it is with everyone born of the Spirit" (John 3:8 NIV). God can put into anyone, at any time, the disposition to move in his direction—by means totally outside our personal trying or our organizational mechanizations.

This does not mean, however, that individuals are passive observers in their own interior redecoration. Spiritual growth begins when God speaks to us, but spiritual growth can continue only as we hear, listen, and act. The formation of Christlikeness in human personality continues only through the commitments we make. If we make no spiritual commitments, we experience little spiritual growth.

Just as spiritual growth often begins in ways outside our personal or ecclesiastical control, it seems to move forward at an unpredictable pace. Sometimes it seems instantaneous. At other times, spiritual growth seems to move like molasses. Overall, one's growth toward spiritual maturity appears to be a series of unpredictable and uncontrollable turning points. At such times (developmental windows and moments of teachability), God becomes real in fresh ways, and people move to new depths of commitment.[10]

Although spiritual growth is primarily a transaction between God's Spirit and the human will, churches do play a role in the process. Sometimes, spiritual growth *begins* in a worship service or during some other church activity. As one person said, "When I attended the first time, I knew I was ready to move in a new direction." After people have connected with God, churches can exert influences that facilitate *continuing* spiritual growth. Church leaders cannot do what God does, but God delegates some roles to them. Through the ideas, methods, and programs that churches use, their potential for helping people grow spiritually can be increased or decreased.

PEOPLE ARE DIFFERENT!

Churches serve a variety of audiences, each at a different age and stage of development. Optimum facilitation of spiritual growth, therefore, does not happen in churches that are like fast-food establishments, serving only one type of spiritual-growth fare. Churches must operate more like the food section in a giant shopping mall—offering everything from tacos to fine dining. There are always some basics. As the Gallup research indicates, Americans most often say that their faith is nourished through prayer, helping others, attending religious services, and reading the Bible.[11] But spiritual growth also happens in many other ways.

During recent years, the renewal of interest in the classic spiritual disciplines of prayer, meditation, and spiritual mentoring may have produced a blind spot. Because of that emphasis, church leaders have paid scant attention to the numerous other ways in which people grow spiritually. This book will describe these other ways—while also addressing the basics—and suggest practical how-to ideas for strengthening their impact. The bottom-line objective is to share proven methods for strengthening a congregation's ability to accomplish its basic business—helping people to grow spiritually.

The research on which I have based this book began during several years of developing spiritual-growth programs across North America. A basic list of seven spiritual-growth factors increased to twelve as the items were tested with various lay and clergy workshop groups. From that point, a questionnaire evolved, which brought responses from several thousand people, in hundreds of congregations of various denominations. Write-in comments added two new items to the list of factors, bringing the total to fourteen.

The following Spiritual Growth Opinion Poll represents my accumulated learning as indicated above. I encourage you to use it with your own congregation. It can provide you with invaluable information as you work toward greater spiritual growth in your church.

Permission is granted to reprint this opinion poll for use in local congregations. Warning: Changing the wording will limit its effectiveness.

SPIRITUAL-GROWTH OPINION POLL

This information-gathering process will help us to determine the directions our church should take in providing spiritual-growth opportunities. You have a limited amount of time, so begin filling it out when you arrive for worship. A quick, feeling-level response is desired, rather than *lengthy* reflection. Early in the service, five minutes of meditative background music will be set aside for completion of the sheet. Ushers will collect them immediately thereafter. Please do not sign your name.

Please check the items that you feel have produced the most spiritual growth in your life:

____ 1. *Worship*—focusing on God and sensing God's presence.

____ 2. *Music*—feeling moved to give God greater attention.

____ 3. *Prayer*—relating to God.

____ 4. *Fellowship*—receiving God's love through others.

____ 5. *Preaching*—hearing God speak to me.

____ 6. *Service*—giving God's love to others through time and talent.

____ 7. *Stewardship*—giving money to help with God's work in the world.

____ 8. *Bible study*—trying to obtain God's guidance for daily living.

____ 9. *Books*—receiving inspiration, information, and motivation.

____10. *Encouragement*—helping others grow spiritually through affirmation, counseling, inclusion, and spiritual mentoring.

____11. *Leadership*—providing vision that helps Christians set goals consistent with God's will, and working together to accomplish God's work in the church and the world.

____12. *Administration*—carrying out and helping others to carry out one or more of the church's ministry tasks.

____13. *Retreats*—experiencing inspiration and insights in a physical setting apart from my daily life and the local church.

____14. *Evangelism*—helping others find God.

____*Other.* Please describe (use reverse side of sheet, if necessary).

I am a (please check one):   My age is (please check one):
____ Very active layperson   ____ 0-19   ____ 45-54
____ Somewhat active layperson   ____ 20-24   ____ 55-64
____ Not very active layperson   ____ 25-34   ____ 65-74
____ Local church clergy   ____ 35-44   ____ 75-84
____ National, regional, district,   ____ 85+
or area staff person

Although not a random sample of clergy, laity, and national leaders, the opinion-poll responders provided representative viewpoints regarding the congregational factors that facilitate personal spiritual growth. These responses gave numerous new insights on which to build both this book's advice and future research. Examples:

1. Because clergy become accustomed to handling holy things, their awareness can dim regarding the power with which they are working. Thus, those most involved in church work can begin to see many spiritual-growth facilitators as merely church work—rather than as God's tools for helping people to grow spiritually.

2. Many people indicate that reading inspirational books that illustrate biblical truths has helped them grow spiritually. These books, though not listed on the original opinion poll, got an incredible number of write-in votes. Bible study—trying to obtain God's guidance for daily living—was on the poll's list. However, the tabulation indicated that many people obtained as much or more spiritual-growth insights from books about the Bible as from the Bible itself. This substantiates researcher George Barna's observation that many people cannot make sense out of the Bible without guidance.[12]

3. In most ways, pastors and laypeople report similar views regarding what causes spiritual growth. At four points, however, they differ greatly!

- While laypeople rank fellowship as number three in importance on the list of spiritual-growth facilitators, clergy cite fellowship as number seven. Does not this "red-flag data" warn clergy that facilitating fellowship is a more important element in their leadership role than they personally believe?

- While laypeople rank retreats number ten on the list of spiritual-growth facilitators, pastors cite retreats as number five. This undoubtedly comes from the fact that clergy are more likely to have attended numerous retreats. As one layperson said, "Haven't tried this, but I think it would

produce spiritual growth." (Does not this difference between clergy and laity tell leaders responsible for spiritual
growth among pastors that they should focus on retreats as
a primary way to accomplish that goal?)

- Stewardship of money seems far more important for laypeople (number seven) than for clergy, who ranked it number
  eleven. Again, personal experiences may determine this
  difference. Laypeople are more likely to see stewardship of
  money as one of their primary means of serving God; clergy
  are more involved in preaching and teaching about the
  stewardship of money.

- Most remarkable, however, is the difference between laypeople and the clergy who serve as denominational leaders in
  national, regional, district, and area structures. These spe-
  cialized leaders rank retreats as number one (compared to
  a number ten ranking by laypeople); they rank worship as
  number five (compared to a number one ranking by laypeople); they rank preaching as number ten (compared to a
  number four ranking by laypeople). As with local clergy, the
  personal experiences of these national clergy give them a
  different viewpoint. The big hazard: These national clergy
  could misconstrue reality by thinking that their personal
  view is "normal"—that is, similar to the experiences that
  help typical laypeople grow spiritually.

4. Birth dates makes some difference in what people say
helps them to grow spiritually:

- Retreats are more important for people age 0–24, doubtless
  because they have more opportunity to attend them.

- Fellowship is more important to people age 25–44 (number
  two in rank) than to people age 45–64 (number four in
  rank).

- Bible study is more important to people age 45–64 (number
  three in rank) than to people age 25–44 (number six in
  rank).

- Service is more important to people age 25–44 (number four in rank) than to people age 45–64, or to people age 65+ (both number six in rank).
- Stewardship is more important to people age 65+ (number five in rank) than to people age 25–44 (number eight in rank) or to people age 45–64 (number seven in rank).
- Evangelism is far more important to people age 65+ (number eight in rank) than to people age 45—64, or to people age 25–44 (both number twelve in rank).
- Retreats are more important to people age 25–44 (number nine in rank) than to people age 45–64 (number eleven in rank) or to people age 65+(number twelve in rank). This is surely due, at least in part, to the fellowship factor. Younger Christians may still clearly remember in a positive way their experiences in youth groups. Young adults ought, therefore, to respond to spiritual-growth retreats sponsored by churches, especially if they are inexpensive and convenient to attend.

Churches that use the revised Spiritual-Growth Opinion Poll can: (a) Bring to the surface insights regarding the way people in a particular congregation best experience spiritual growth; (b) motivate people who complete the poll on Sunday morning to consider the ways they need to be saying yes to God's call to spiritual growth; and (c) help pastors and key lay leaders to better detect their personal blind spots—the spiritual-growth facilitators that are important to most members of their congregation but not to them personally.

Many people will check all the spiritual-growth facilitators. As one person said, "All play their important role in my formation." As another person said, "The usefulness of any depends upon a person's individual needs at any specific time." The field must be ready for the seed.

Two elements work together to determine the power of any of these fourteen spiritual-growth facilitators:

1. *One element is availability.* We cannot use what churches do not make available.

2. *The other element is receptivity.* Individuals are not equally receptive at all times in their lives. A spiritual-growth facilitator's availability in a congregation is irrelevant until the individual becomes receptive.

The fourteen facilitators are treated in the remaining chapters of this book in an order similar to their overall ranking by lay and clergy opinion-poll respondents of all ages: worship, music, prayer, fellowship, preaching, service and stewardship, Bible study and other reading, encouragement, leadership and administration, retreats, and evangelism.

This ranking does not, however, mean that the last chapters of this book contain unimportant items; every item is important to some persons. The sequence of the chapters does, however, mean that more people believed that the items in the earlier chapters helped them to grow spiritually, while fewer persons felt they were helped by the items in the later chapters.

FOLLOWERSHIP

Only once in the Gospels did Jesus say, "Be born again" (John 3:3 KJV). More than thirty times, he said, "Follow me." And yet, churches often seem to teach that being born again is more important than following.

How do we follow effectively? Primarily, through experiences that produce spiritual growth. How do congregations provide those experiences? Primarily, through the fourteen ways listed above. How do congregations increase the effectiveness of these fourteen spiritual-growth facilitators? By recognizing their value and becoming much more intentional about providing them.

When a small boy focused a magnifying glass on some dead leaves momentarily, they burst into flame. The glass contained no fire, but it focused the sun's rays in a way that caused a powerful transformation in the leaves. The fourteen factors that increase spiritual growth contain no magic. But by holding the "glass" right, these methods increase the flame of spiritual growth ignited by the Spirit. When churches provide people with opportunities to engage in these experiences, the Son's fire, through the rays of the Holy Spirit, sets them aflame.

Chapter 3

WORSHIP IS
JOB ONE

At the time, no one noticed that May 24, 1738, was a hinge of history for England and America. Because of what happened that day, an obscure young man would leave sizable footprints in the secular and religious culture of both continents. That May day was not the first stage in his development. He had participated in the Holy Club at Lincoln College, Oxford. He had served as a missionary in the colony of Georgia (1736–1738). Yet, biographers would compare his earlier spiritual experiences to this one as like five-watt bulbs dimmed by stadium lights. John Wesley's empowering moment of spiritual growth came during a worship service at Aldersgate, a small English church.

Worship, like air, is so prevalent in American life that we can miss its significance. Because dramatic spiritual growth does not happen to everyone each time a person worships, we tend to overlook its value. *But when given the opportunity to choose from a list of twelve factors that helped them to grow spiritually, church members and attenders checked worship more frequently than any other item.* An Old Testament prophet said, "You will seek me and find me when you seek me with all your heart" (Jer. 29:13 NIV). That happens more often in worship than elsewhere. Airplanes inhabit spaces other than airports, but that is a good place to go if you want to board one. Likewise, worship increases our chances of a close encounter with God.

Why is worship such a powerful means of connecting with God? Because we are more likely to concentrate our mind's attention on God here than in any other set of circumstances. We cannot talk with God and listen to God until we pay attention to God. Worship helps us to build a bridge of attention, thus allowing more traffic to cross from both directions. This makes worship the primary ministry tool of every congregation. Job one of the Church is not pastoral care, or helping the needy, or changing societal/governmental structures, or missions. The first business of the Church is to help people connect with God and grow spiritually. Worship is the number-one way this happens. After two thousand years, a church's most powerful program is still its worship service.

There is a sign on a school building in a poverty area in south Texas, near the Mexico border: "Garriga Elementary." Under the name is the slogan: "Where Success Begins." Worship is the elementary school of spiritual growth; it does not end here, but for most people it begins here. What happens in other ways and places builds on this foundation.

INTERIOR-DECORATING CLASSES

People obviously believe that worship helps them. Otherwise, why would more Americans be in church every month than go to vote in presidential elections every four years? Why would more Americans attend worship services in a single month than attend any sports event during the entire year?[1] But how, exactly, does worship help?

The short answer to that question: People believe worship strengthens, repairs, and refocuses their lives. The long answer: Worship benefits people in at least ten ways.

1. **Worship dispels loneliness.** It helps to erase the feeling of disconnectedness that counselors say is one of the most universally reported stresses of contemporary society.

2. **Worship brings hope.** Research indicates that public worship attendance correlates with life satisfaction.[2] That data

is surely related to worship's ability to give people a different perspective. Worship helps us to see over the wall of circumstances that restrict our vision.

3. **Worship counters self-centeredness.** One of the best ways to define the biblical word *sin* is "self-centeredness"—which leads inevitably to the internal conviction that I am my own God. By attending worship, we move beyond that self-reverence. God, rather than self, becomes the focus of self.

4. **Worship reminds us of important values we tend to forget.** A student's thinking improves in the presence of an excellent teacher. Thinking in God's presence forms *character,* the central assembly line of human personality. Character manufactures all our *values*—such as: (a) the importance of loving people, rather than things; (b) the importance of forgiving, rather than resenting; and (c) the importance of serving, rather than seeking only to be served.

5. **Worship strengthens courage.** Someone flying over the North Atlantic Sea noted that the small icebergs move in one direction, while the large icebergs move in the opposite direction. This happens because the surface winds drive the small ones, but the deep ocean currents move the huge ones.[3] Worship, by keeping us in touch with the deep currents, often helps us move against life's strong surface winds. "Those who wait for the Lord shall renew their strength, they shall mount up with wings like eagles, they shall run and not be weary, they shall walk and not faint" (Isa. 40:31).

6. **Worship gives us the opportunity to express thanksgiving.** "Praise God from whom all blessings flow" has retained its popularity as a worship response because it is among the most basic instincts of human nature. When Noah stepped out of the ark, he had plenty to do. He had to construct shelter for the family. The cattle needed care. But Noah's first act was to build an altar and worship. We are tempted to reverse that pattern, putting work ahead of worship. That reversal draws us back into the powerful Bermuda Triangle of thinking that we alone are responsible for all the good things that happen

to us. Thanksgiving in worship is a powerful antidote for the poison of self-sufficiency.

7. **Worship brings us a sense of forgiveness.** People can recognize their self-centeredness, but they cannot get on the other side of it by themselves. Worship moves us beyond our limited psychological ability to emotionally let go of dangerous fixations on our imperfections and failures.

8. **Worship renews our faith.** Studies indicate that within seven days, we human beings forget approximately 93 percent of what we learn. Our mental computers therefore require repeated reprogramming. Perhaps that is why the Bible suggests that we worship every seven days.

9. **Worship is a transcendent experience which helps God call us out of what we are to what we are yet to become.** A book about contemporary evangelism lists sixteen steps between the stage of superficial awareness of God and that of becoming Christlike. The insight needed for taking the next of any of these steps is found most often in worship.

10. **Worship is a highly organized form of corporate prayer that brings positive change to people.** Sir Isaac Newton's First Law of Motion says that a body tends to keep in motion when it is in motion, and it tends to stay at rest when it is at rest—unless acted upon by some external force. That law of physics also applies to humanity. We tend to continue in whatever state we are in, until we are influenced by forces outside ourselves. Worship enables us to pay attention, so that God can strengthen, repair, and refocus our lives.

WHAT INGREDIENTS
MAKE WORSHIP EFFECTIVE?

In the centuries before Christ, Old Testament temple worship included sacrifice, prayer, music, and dancing (II Chron. 29:27; II Sam. 6:14; Pss. 149:3 and 150:4). This involved adoration (Ps. 99:5), praise (Ps. 34:3), thanksgiving (Pss. 103:2 and 107:8), confession (Ps. 38:18), seeking God's presence

(Ps. 42:1*ff.*), and humble consecration (Ps. 119:10). As the synagogues became worship centers alongside temple worship during the fifth century B.C., Scripture reading was added to the list, making God's requirements known.

Since many of the first-century Christians were Jews, the New Testament house churches modeled their worship on that of Jewish synagogues, which were scattered throughout major cities of the ancient world. In these synagogues, worshiping God "in spirit and truth" (John 4:23, 24) had already replaced the animal sacrifices of Old Testament temple days. To this evolving pattern, Christians added the breaking of bread (Acts 20:7, 11), based on the symbolism of: (1) Old Testament animal sacrifice; (2) the Exodus of the migrating Hebrews from slavery in Egypt in approximately 1290–1224 B.C.; (3) Jesus' last supper with his disciples (I Cor. 11:23*ff.*); and (4) the believer receiving the Spirit of Christ (John 6:53*ff.*).

Worship that helps people grow spiritually stands on that biblical foundation. It contains praise, self-assessment, confession, assurance, forgiveness, proclamation, teaching, vision, and opportunity for commitment. Yet, spiritually maturing worship contains no central core of forms or practices. Both "high church" liturgical and "low church" nonliturgical services can provide these basic, spiritually enriching elements. Factors that make the most difference in promoting spirituality relate more to style than to form.

Worship, in some respects, is like ice skating. In Olympic competition, skaters are scored in two categories—technical merit and style—what they do and how they do it. Worship is the same. It contains technical elements, and it has style. There are a limited number of actions from which worship leaders can select what they do. Thus, worship style is usually a more powerful determiner of worship effectiveness.

If we want our worship services to spiritually enrich lives, the following questions can start us down that road. (See the

Resource Section for workshops that provide greater detail in effective worship methods.)

1. **Does our worship focus on God?** Authentic worship has an authentic object. The root of the English word *worship* is "worthship." Christian worship declares the worthship of God. Other kinds of worship declare the worthship of something else. Without consciously intending to, we can make fatal substitutions in designing a worship service. We can substitute the worthship of tradition for the worship of God. We can substitute the worthship of psychology. Worship that does not begin and continue with God as its central focus becomes something other than Christian worship.

One of the pastors in a Pennsylvania church walks through the congregation gathering cards that contain prayer petitions. These are included in the time of pastoral prayer and then placed on the communion table. This action demonstrates that God, not some other object, is the center of worship.

2. **Is our worship service people-oriented?** A news item from Selma, Alabama, reported that dull worship services have led to an exodus of African American members from the Lutheran Church, Missouri Synod, in that area. "German music is just not attuned to what many of us are accustomed to and grew up with," said the Reverend Ulmer Marshall, pastor of an African American congregation in Mobile.[4]

Pastor Marshall was saying that his denomination's customary worship style does not communicate with real people in that culture. We can easily see why this might happen, as Germanic Lutherans try to communicate with African American black southerners. But we may experience greater difficulty in seeing that exactly the same thing can happen in Anglo congregations. Without realizing it, churches can substitute a liturgy that spoke to people two centuries ago—or worship elements that spoke to young adults in the 1950s.

Effective worship is incarnational. Why did God come to the world of people in the form of a person? Because that was the only way God could get through to people. Effective worship is user-friendly. It communicates with real people who live in this present time and this present space—not some other time or some other place. Being incarnational does not mean that we accommodate ourselves to every passing fad of our culture. But incarnational worship focuses on building a bridge between *these people* and God, not between *some other people,* some other time, and God.

Failing to accommodate our worship style to the present cultural expressions of people in our community is the height of arrogance! This means that we are unwilling to do what God was willing to do—humble himself and show up in a Bethlehem stable. It also means that we fail to communicate with people in ways that make a difference—that we fail at the essential definition of the word *priest*—"bridge builder."

3. **Is our worship service real-life oriented?** Someone said that people who deliver sermons should stand with one foot in the Bible and one foot on the sidewalk. That principle also applies to people who plan worship services.

Twice a year, include a 3 X 5 card in each worship bulletin. Ask members to list three issues they struggle with in trying to apply the Christian faith to their lives. Explain that you will use these responses in the planning of worship and sermons during the next few months. More people will look forward to a relevant service or sermon (and the curious will enjoy finding out what problems other people have).[5]

4. **Do we plan the parts of the service as carefully as the pastor plans the parts of the sermon?** In a Texas congregation, the pastor and a staff person meet each Tuesday morning with members of the worship committee and the choir director to: (a) finalize plans for the coming Sunday; and (b) brainstorm ideas for future Sundays. Not every church will want to formalize its plans in this way. But churches with effective worship have pastors who give equal attention to the sermon and the other elements of worship. Failure to attain that balance

produces, at best, a diamond set in a plastic band—and at worst, a piece of cut glass in a plastic band.

How can we know how the parts of the service speak to people in our community? Ask! Do some basic research into the way our worship service communicates with and meets the spiritual needs of members. Do a morning-worship survey, using the following questions: (a) What parts of our worship service are the most meaningful to you personally? (b) What parts of our worship service are not very meaningful to you personally? (c) What do you feel would make our worship service more meaningful to you personally? (d) Is there anything else that you have been wanting to tell someone about our worship service? The questionnaire should provide a set of blanks to check, whereby people can indicate the decade in which they were born. Do not ask them to sign their names.

5. **Do we view worship as a drama in which the worshipers are actors, rather than a drama in which the worshipers are observers?** The difference between "performance worship" and "participant worship" approximates the the difference between looking at an excellent steak and eating it. The percentage of repeat customers at those two types of restaurants is also approximately the same. We call the crowd that gathers on Sunday morning a "congregation," rather than an "audience." If we change that definition by the way we plan worship, we change the number of people who show up. The pastor of a fast-growing United Church of Christ congregation in Illinois says that their worshipers participate twelve to fifteen times during each service; yet they sing only once from the hymnal. Count! How many times do your worshipers actually participate in concrete ways during the service? In most churches, increasing that number increases the value of the service for the worshiper. Effective worship is not a spectator sport.

Participation Possibilities:

- In one church, as the children come forward in preparation for the children's sermon, the congregation sings, "Jesus Loves the Little Children."
- In another congregation, as the children leave for children's church about one-third of the way through the service, the people sing, "I've Got the Joy, Joy, Joy, Joy Down in My Heart." For some, this joy may have a double meaning. But the participation adds a touch of celebration to what, in most churches, is a dead spot.

6. **Do we maintain a balance in the experiential tools we expect people to use in worship participation?** People connect with God through worship in these five ways:

- Sensory (sight, hearing, smell, touch, taste)
- Emotional (symbolism and feeling)
- Rational (memory and logic)
- Spiritual (mystery and imagination)
- Actional (speech and movement)

People are different in this regard. Different generations also find different experiential tools helpful. For example, young adults are accustomed to experiences that include sounds, sights, ideas, emotions, and information in one package. Older adults were raised in a different environment. Balance is therefore the key to communicating with both generations in the same service.

7. **Does our worship service communicate with contemporary young adults in the twenty-five to forty-five age range?** Older adults naturally expect younger adults to have a meaningful worship experience under the same circumstances they did when they were that age. At some stages of history, this has been true. However, for at least two-thirds of younger adults, it is not true now. This misperception is a major source of ineffective worship services. The differences are so subtle, however, that even the best of pastors often fail to see them.

People born before 1946 define meaningful worship in terms of reverence and solemnity. People born after 1946 define meaningful worship in terms of self-expression, active participation, and a heart-felt exuberance that includes warmth, spontaneity, enthusiasm, and vitality. Since the 28 percent of Americans born before 1946 are more likely to control the style of worship in their church, these leaders must be superintentional in trying to achieve balance. Many of the 47 percent of Americans born between 1946 and 1976 are now returning to church. If the worship service feels antique, they do not stick.

8. **Do we recognize the value of multiple worship services?** Some churches attempt to reach both older and younger adults by adding another Sunday morning service. This allows for a different worship style. Some older adults object to this. But the parents of Baby Boomers (born between 1946 and 1964) and the grandparents of Baby Busters (born since 1964) did exactly the same thing during the 1950s, though in a different way. They started thousands of new suburban churches in the 1940s and 1950s post-war era, in which they did things differently because they were serving a different generation. They started new services, too, but usually in new buildings, so nobody viewed those new services as a radical change.

9. **Is the format contemporary?** Worship in the 1950s was tied to a standard format that seldom changed; it focused on listening to the choir, special music, and a topical sermon. Worship in contemporary growing churches is more likely to contain many variations each week, depending upon the theme of the message. It may include drama, interviews, or visual aids. Bill Hybels, pastor of the fifteen thousand people who attend worship at Willow Creek Community Church in the northwest Chicago suburbs, says, "This is the generation that grew up on television . . . you have to present religion to them in a creative and visual way."[6]

The major change in format usually involves: (a) high congregational participation early in the service; and (b) a much greater emphasis on beginning with enthusiasm and energy, rather than with solemnity and quiet meditation. The service contains the same general parts each week, but the worshiper gets an overall feeling of liveliness and creativity, rather than solemn sameness. Both tradition and innovation are present, and sometimes intermingled.

10. **Is the worship pace consistent with the expectations of most young adults?** Effective pace does not mean "rushed." Rather, it means that the service communicates momentum and contains little dead time. The demand for a faster pace applies to everything in the service—music, prayers, liturgy, announcements, preaching. The pace acceptable to young adults in 1975 is perceived as dull, slow, and boring to most persons of that age group now, one-third of a century later. Nothing happens slowly anymore.

In 1968, the average length of a network news "sound byte" from a presidential candidate was 42.3 seconds; in 1988, it was 9.8 seconds.[7] American television producers hold each frame for two seconds. In England, the frame time is three to five seconds, which tells us something about the American "threshold of boredom." Watching ushers amble down the aisle, or watching a soloist walk toward the microphone can cause contemporary worshipers to lose their attention focus. Many of them change mental channels and think about other things.

11. **Is the worship atmosphere warm and friendly?** People who come to worship God also want to connect in a positive way with other people. When that fails to happen, their worship experience feels seriously compromised. Thus, the time-worn words that express one of the greatest condemnations of a worship service: "Not a soul spoke to me!"

The opposite is captured in the statement from a Baby Boomer when he first attended Calvary Chapel in Costa Mesa, California: "I felt an abundant flow of love the moment I walked through the door. There was not even a fleeting hint of judgmentalism here. Rather, I felt a terrific sense of belonging."[8] He was saying what many researchers are observing: Contemporary people seek churches that are caring places, not merely teaching spaces.

Yet, most young-adult visitors prefer not to be introduced in the worship service. They want the worship-service attenders to be friendly, but they want to remain anonymous among the total crowd. Ritual of Friendship Pads that provide information are fine with most of them, but being introduced is not. They seem to be looking for warm, friendly anonymity. Young adults do, however, respond well to the atmosphere created when worshipers share "joys and concerns." This adds a dimension of warmth, caring, and humanity that most of them appreciate.

12. **Does the service contain sufficient change and variety each week?** Worshipers in plateaued and declining membership congregations indicate that their services are sometimes, or frequently, characterized by monotony, boredom, and formality. By contrast, worship in growing churches is characterized by spontaneity and variety. Apparently, for unchurched persons who have relatively little motivation to attend worship, boring and overly predictable services reinforce the reasons they stopped attending church in the first place.[9]

All human beings need a balance between security and stimulation in their experiences. What do we say when we leave on vacation? "I sure am glad to get away!" What do we say when we return from a vacation? "It sure is good to be home!" People have these same needs when they worship. They need the security of the familiar, but they also need the stimulation of variety. In the 1950s, our needs tilted more toward *security*. In the 1990s, our needs tilt more toward *variety*. Why? World War II created an age of anxiety. Television created an age of boredom.

13. **Does the room in which worship occurs contribute positively to the objective of communicating with God?** Several factors influence whether a sanctuary encourages a God conversation: Is it well lighted? Is the sound system of good quality? Does it seem to be a celebration center, focused on something beyond human experience? Or does it feel like a museum or a mausoleum? Is it decorated in a way that joyfully points toward God, or does it look more like an airplane hangar? Even in the first unit of a new congregation, colorful, changeable banners can brighten the sanctuary personality. Especially in large congregations that plan to serve many Baby Boomers and Baby Busters, shabby worship areas decrease spiritual pulling and growing power.

14. **Do we recognize that planning and leading worship is an incredibly difficult art?** Because of its deep traditional, cultural, and emotional roots in the human psyche, trying to improve worship patterns is tricky business. Peggy Noonan, famous speech writer for President Reagan, said that since everyone can write—they learn how in grade school—they usually think they can write pretty well and have difficulty in judging their own work. When an expert tells them that they do not write well, they are suspicious of that judgment and often resentful.[10]

Her insight applies also to worship. Every church has worship services, and most people think theirs is pretty good. They are so accustomed to it that they have difficulty realizing the truth of what other people tell them about it. Trying to improve anyone's worship service is therefore a dangerous business—subject to misunderstanding and running aground on the sandbars of deeply held opinions. However, it is a necessary business. Worship quality determines the traffic capacity of the primary communication bridges between Jesus, the Christ, and the people who want to enter his spiritual kingdom.

WARNING: HIGH VOLTAGE

A building at 220 East Main Street in Olney, Texas, carries large stone letters across its front: ENERGY BUILDING. When a church operates at optimum effectiveness, that sign could fit on its sanctuary. Worship is where we find much of the spiritual energy necessary to follow Christ in daily discipleship. Without effective worship, discipleship loses its voltage. If there is any single thing likely to energize both the vitality of a church and the spiritual lives of its people, that one thing is worship.

Chapter 4

JOYFUL NOISES

I soon gave up going to that church," he said. "It was a gloomy place. There was no joy."

"What made it feel that way?" the consultant asked.

"A lot of it was the music," the man replied. "It was like attending a funeral every Sunday!" That observation is one of the most frequently expressed insights regarding American church life. Yet, it also seems to qualify as one of the least frequently *heard* and acted upon by church leaders.

Contemporary Americans consistently rank music slightly above preaching as a spiritual-growth facilitator. In the opinion poll that formed the foundation for this book, worship music was not one of the twelve original items. *But numerous write-in votes, such as the following, demanded a position for music on the final list:*

- Music—for me, a direct connection to God, love, and creativity.
- Worship hymns that raise the spirit.
- Music, relating to the worship experience—the expression of love and praise through note and sound.
- Music in worship. I throughly enjoy the organ, piano, choirs, and congregational hymn singing.
- Music—a good music program can do so much for a church. Young and old can be drawn by music.

One pastor says that in order of importance, effective worship involves music, preaching, and caring. Much evidence indicates that she is right. Researcher C. Kirk Hadaway found that 90 percent of large, growing churches rate their music program as excellent or good, compared to 53 percent of declining churches.[1] Among smaller congregations, 65 percent of growing churches rate their music program as excellent or good, compared to 35 percent of declining churches. Music is approximately 40 percent of any service, and it helps to set the tone for everything else. Joy and hope are important aspects of God's nature. Music helps raise people to that level of consciousness.

Why does music now seem so much more important as a spiritual-growth facilitator than it did in earlier years? Probably because, in recent decades, music has become a far more pervasive aspect of life. The number of gold records awarded in 1961 for albums selling a million copies was 15; in 1971, 91; in 1991, 217.[2] That increase far exceeds American population growth. From the earliest moments of life to the grave, music influences us. We absorb almost as much music as air.

Despite all the evidence, however, complaints about ineffective worship music consistently rank near the top on congregational opinion polls. Why can church leaders not seem to hear insights regarding the kinds of music that help people to grow spiritually? Among the several reasons, three are especially important: (1) Pastors—whose life experiences involve large doses of seminary training, and ten to twenty hours per week of sermon preparation—have trouble believing that the Word can come through channels other than the preached word; (2) Musically trained leaders—whose professional education usually builds into their psyche deep preferences and prejudices regarding particular types of music—have trouble realizing that the Word can come through channels other than the kind of music they personally prefer; (3) Lay leaders—whose music preferences are formed in their teen and young-adult years, in a particular decade, congregation, and denomination—have trouble seeing that the Word can come through other music channels. Because of those three perceptual barricades, few church leaders take action on the complaints they hear.

WHY IS MUSIC POWERFUL?

How well would a movie come across without a musical background? Would that affect its quality? What if the soundtrack played the "Star Spangled Banner" over and over throughout the movie? What if music backgrounds were picked at random, with no thought to whether they matched the movie's message? These imaginary scenarios illustrate the powerful role that music plays in communication. Music helps to connect our emotions to our intellect, our feelings to our thinking, our will to our knowledge, our inclinations to our information.

Life without feeling is less than life. Without appropriate music, words from God can sound like dull thuds, rather than the silver bells of new possibilities. Music conveys truth in a way that we can internalize and remember. Poetic and metaphoric language enables hymns to deepen our insight in ways not possible through prose and stories alone. Whether singing in the shower or in a church, we are grappling with, assimilating, and expressing ideas that powerfully influence our lives. Song is the voice of the human spirit at its deepest level.

A rabbinical story tells of the moment Adam first opened his eyes. He looked at creation, and he said to God, "This is utterly fantastic!"

"I know," said God.

"But tell me," Adam asked, "what is the meaning of it all?"

God, taken aback, replied, "You mean it has to have meaning?"

"Of course," Adam answered.

"Well, I am sure you will think of something," God said, and sauntered off.[3]

Understanding the meaning of life and faith is complex. Communicating that meaning is even more challenging. Music is one of the best tools for accomplishing that communication. Thus the psalmist said, "Make a joyful noise to the Lord, all the earth. Worship the Lord with gladness; come into his presence with singing" (Ps. 100:1-2). In music, we say the unsayable, know the unfathomable, and feel with conviction what we cannot comprehend. In music, we experience the joy of life at its fullest. In effective worship music, we connect with God.

WORSHIP MUSIC ANATOMY

What kinds of music are effective in helping people to connect with God? That is almost like asking a physician what makes human anatomy work. Reporting the *results* of "what works" in worship music is easier than analyzing the parts— just as observing an Olympic gold-medal diver is far easier than describing the way the diver's bones and muscles work together. In worship music, the complexity of the answer multiplies tenfold. The type of music that helps young adults to experience God's presence and receive God's Word for their lives has changed. It differs from the kind of music older adults found meaningful when they were that age.

Church music in the 1950s was built on a foundation of solemn, stately hymns, accompanied by piano or organ. The choir director focused on the choir. In growing churches today, music is often built on the foundation of praise songs, sung with gusto and often accompanied by guitars and a variety of other instruments. The music director focuses on involving the entire congregation, not just the choir, in worshiping God through song. Music often accompanies the Scripture reading, the prayers, and sometimes even the close of the message.

The words of the "praise songs" used by many growing congregations are often taken from the Bible and address God directly, rather than speaking about God. To some older adults, these songs sound like choruses from their summer-camp years. However, most of these verses are younger than the Baby Boomers who love to sing them in worship. Most of the mainline churches that use these contemporary praise songs do not, however, use them as their only hymns. They blend in the more traditional hymns, so as to meet the spiritual needs of all age groups.

This blending is essential, since every congregation, every Sunday morning, contains three types of people, with three different music preferences: Some worshipers, many of whom have birth dates prior to 1927, connect with God best through "the old gospel hymns" (most of which were written between 1900 and 1935). Most of the second group were born between 1927 and 1946, and they like the classic hymns of the church (many of which were written 200 to 300 years ago). These great hymns, of which "The Church's One Foundation" is an example, predominated in growing churches of the 1940s and 1950s. Still another group, most of whom have birth dates on this side of 1946, likes hymns written or set to a different tune since 1960. Many of these young adults also enjoy the contemporary choral responses more than the traditional, centuries-old responses.

More than anything else, birth dates determine the type of music that helps people to connect with God. Music preferences, solidified primarily in the teen years and early twenties, do not bend easily. Their owners, even when they recognize their prejudices, can change them about as easily as they can change their genetic codes. Most of the time, however, they do not even know they possess these prejudices.

People who wear glasses or contact lenses see the world in a particular way because of the way their lenses are ground. Soon they become unaware of their lenses, unconsciously using them to interpret reality. Likewise, almost every worshiper interprets music through the lenses of his or her generational experiences. When people say, "I like the great old classic hymns of the church," they usually think that they are telling you about quality music. But they are really reporting their birth dates, which largely determine the kind of lenses they wear.

Music is more feeling than thinking, more emotional than rational. Feelings are built into personality at levels far deeper than thoughts. Thoughts can be quickly educated (changed) by adding information. Feelings are educated (changed) more slowly, and more through personal experiences than through new data. That is why the church's music department is sometimes called the "war department." People are discussing reality by looking at the same thing through different lenses, usually without knowing it.

Church music is both emotional and rational, but it far exceeds the boundaries of either, and the total of both. Music is rational (all sensory input is processed by the mind). Music is emotional (few inputs more powerfully and quickly influence our mood and attitude). But music takes us to a place beyond emotion and thinking. Music evokes feelings by reaching into our memories through the rational and imaginative levels of our beings. This moves us into the *spiritual planes of experience*—where God can speak to us in ways not otherwise possible. Music (a) tells the story of faith; (b) strengthens personal faith; and (c) bonds worshipers together in ways that pulpit words cannot accomplish. Small wonder, then, that people fight over the kind of music a church should use. They sincerely feel that the type of music that helps them connect with God will surely help others, too.

In churches that serve the spiritual needs of every age group, the music leaders understand the different lenses that people wear on Sunday morning. These leaders strive for balance in their selection of hymns and music. They understand the futility of attempting to set up an optical shop which tries to regrind lenses by organizing fifty-two music-appreciation courses each year. Thus, a contemporary researcher recommends that leaders add "a healthy dose of tasteful contemporary Christian gospel along with more traditional church music."[4]

Other leaders suggest an intentional "formula," which each week uses (1) a traditional "classic" hymn; (2) a gospel-era hymn; (3) a hymn or chorus from the contemporary music scene; and (4) one or more contemporary "responses." In this process, the leaders retain sensitivity to their denomination's traditions, while recognizing the generalized differences in the way we meet the spiritual needs of worshipers.

Balance in hymn type is not the only issue in church music. The following questions can assist leaders in evaluating several other spiritual-growth-facilitating qualities in worship music.

1. **Do we use familiar hymns?** Worship attenders often complain about hymn selection and the consequent poor participation in congregational singing. Several factors underlie this irritation: (a) People think hymn singing is an important aspect of their worship experience; (b) half of the worshipers who sing think they do not do it well; (c) almost half the people who sing do not read music;[5] and (d) one-third to two-thirds of the people in every congregation in the United States have joined since 1980 from some other denominational family. Because of this new "denominational switching ecumenism," church leaders cannot expect the same familiarity with hymns that they enjoyed three decades ago.

Poor communication between the persons who pick the hymns and those who sing them is natural. They approach the issue from opposite directions. Musicians and staff members pick hymns that seem to complement their theme for the day, their concept of good worship music, and their convictions regarding good worship design. Pew sitters, by contrast, want to sing familiar hymns that allow them to participate in worship.

This conflict in perspective between worshipers and worship leaders reached its zenith in A.D. 364: The Council of Laodicea decreed that only the clergy could sing during the official liturgy. A thousand years passed before the pendulum swung the other way: In the early 1500s, Martin Luther took the side of the pew people, fighting to end the clergy's monopoly on music in worship. By writing thirty-six hymns—many of them set to familiar barroom tunes—he encouraged congregations to respond to God's Word with song.[6] The conflict continues, but in a different way. Worship leaders want to sing "good hymns"; worshipers define good hymns as "hymns I enjoy singing."

Action Possibilities:

• Appoint a task force of twelve persons, evenly distributed across the age range of twenty through eighty. Ask this group to meet once or twice and go through the hymnbook. With each hymn, ask, "Do you know this hymn?" If nine out of the twelve members know the hymn, most of the congregation probably does. If fewer than nine know the hymn, many of the worshipers will have a tough time singing it. From this procedure, compile a list titled "All the Hymns We Presently Know." Take this list to whoever selects the hymns for each Sunday. In some churches, the pastor chooses. In other churches, choices are determined by the choir director, the organist, or the worship committee chair. Threaten whomever it is with potential loss of life or limb if the list is not used.

• Teach new hymns *intentionally*, perhaps with a "hymn of the month" every other month. This protects leaders from trying to teach unfamiliar hymns *accidentally*, and always failing.

• By using a "Favorite Hymn Survey," determine the congregation's top ten or fifteen favorites. Include those in the worship service whenever they fit the theme of that day.

• Are several familiar and favorite hymns absent from the congregation's worship hymnal? Overcome this handicap by printing them on a bulletin-insert sheet. (See the Resource Section for inexpensive ways to obtain copyright permission.)

2. **Is the tempo of our worship music upbeat and fast-moving?** This is another commonly heard complaint about worship music: "Why is the tempo so slow? Can't we pick it up a little?" Familiarity and variety are not enough if the pace drags.

Action Possibility:

• Ask the organist to select five people from the congregation (not choir members) to help monitor this. Select these persons from a broad age range (20 to 70). About once a month, immediately after morning worship, the organist meets with this group for five minutes, and asks, "How is the tempo going?"

3. **Do we use a wide variety of musical instruments in worship?** The Edict of Milan (A.D. 313) banned instrumental music, believing that pagan influences might infiltrate sacred worship.[7] That prohibition did not permanently stick. In the late 1800s, church orchestras were common. These gradually disappeared, however, and by 1950, instruments other than piano or organ were deemed in "questionable taste" by many older leaders.

The 1960s changed that. The musical revolution in secular life brought faster, rhythmic tunes and different instruments into prominence. This change inevitably influenced what young adults find spiritually enriching in worship. Thus, churches that attract large numbers of twenty- and thirty-year-olds often feature guitar, saxophone, and even drums. The orchestras of the late 1800s are back, but with greater variety, including brass ensembles and dance-band combinations.

Many churches are moving back to the piano for some of their worship elements, and some are making use of synthesizers. The pastor of one church, where the average attendance increased from 65 to 147 in one year, says that the worship leaders use the piano, organ, and guitar every Sunday. Musicians who project the impression that the organ is the only pipe the Holy Spirit ever blows will find themselves very lonely in worship. Many of their young adults will migrate to more contemporary worship climates.[8]

4. **Do we recognize that multiple choirs—especially youth choirs, children's choirs, and handbell choirs—strengthen worship attendance and quality, evangelistic effectiveness, and congregational participation?** Generally speaking, churches should organize two musical groups for each 100 average worship attenders. A church averaging an attendance of 200, for example, should have four musical groups—an adult choir, a children's choir, a youth choir, and perhaps a handbell choir. (See the Resource Section for tools to help develop youth and children's choirs.)

Action Possibilities:

- To increase the size of the adult choir, begin by improving the choir's "social climate." Most choirs that grow and remain large are social institutions, not just singing organizations. They have occasional social events, much like those held by large Sunday school classes. Their year usually begins with such an event, to which they invite potential new choir members. Strong choirs give little thought to making church members feel guilty because they do not sing in the choir. Rather, choir members emphasize the enjoyment of choir participation.

- As another productive way to increase the adult choir size, schedule a special Easter or Christmas musical production. Choir leaders recruit several persons from the congregation to help produce the program—with approximately eight weeks of practice prior to the event. People with singing ability usually are willing to make that sort of short-term commitment. And some of them, after becoming socially involved with the choir for this brief period, will join on a full-time basis.

One unusual phenomenon deserves special mention. Despite all efforts to apply the principles listed above, a few congregations develop a "dedicated passivity" regarding hymn singing—meaning that as many as half the worshipers do not participate. Churches of this type must have strong encouragement in order to change these habits. They usually benefit from having someone lead the congregation in singing. Occasional use of the piano, rather than the organ, can sometimes help. And the children's choir, when the children involve the congregation in singing, can have value. Passive adults are more likely to change their patterns when asked to sing with the children.

A RE-CREATIONAL ACTIVITY

In a best-selling novel, *The Evening News* by Arthur Hailey, one of the characters talks about the old 78 RPM records of World War II days. Music from the big bands—Bennie Goodman, Tommy Dorsey, Glenn Miller—accompanied by popular singers of that day—young Frank Sinatra, Ray Eberle, Dick Haymes, the Andrews Sisters—went everywhere the armed forces went. The 78 records were extremely breakable, so they were transported with great care. One of the records, for example, spoke of "seeing you in all the old familiar places." During those arduous times, songs spoke to people as nothing else could.[9]

Music has a *re-creating* power. Through the process of imagination that comes from both rational thinking and emotional feeling—but transcends both—music can bring us to a state of mind, being, and experience not otherwise possible. When people say they like a certain type of worship music, they are saying, "That music creates and re-creates in me something that is not otherwise possible!" Churches that help people grow spiritually find that music is one of their major tools.

Chapter 5

KEEPING IN TOUCH

A little girl went next door, where the neighboring farmer was selling watermelons at a roadside stand. When she picked out a huge watermelon, the farmer said, "That's $3.00."

"I've only got thirty cents," the girl said.

Pointing to a tiny melon in the field near the highway, the farmer asked, "How about that one?"

"I'll take it," she replied, "but leave it on the vine. I'll be back for it in a month" (*Bits & Pieces*).

That watermelon is like many other living organisms. When connected to nourishing roots, they appreciate in value. When disconnected, they die or rot, rather than grow.

Prayer is one of the primary ways people can stay connected to God and grow spiritually. They make their initial connection by turning their attention toward God and that happens in various ways. However, they stay connected by experiencing God in the same way Jesus did: "In the morning, while it was still very dark, he got up and went out to a deserted place, and there he prayed" (Mark 1:35). Through his daily prayer connection, Jesus found the power to be God's person and to do God's will.

Jesus' first disciples eventually learned that basic lesson. They attained more spiritual power through prayer at Pentecost than they had possessed in three years of traveling with

Jesus (Acts 2:1-4). Contemporary disciples report similar experiences. One man described his primary source of spiritual growth this way: "Taking the time to regularly spend time in prayer, a time when I go beyond my comfortable routine." Someone else said, "I was skeptical about prayer, but when I started practicing it every day, a new energy came into my life. God is energy and creativity, and prayer is the way you tune in." *After worship and music, opinion-poll respondents listed prayer as the most powerful means of growing spiritually.*

Many people think that prayer's primary purpose is to receive things they want. Not so! The best thing we receive through prayer is not a thing—it is God. When we pray, we invite the presence and power of God into our minds. Matthew announced the Bethlehem event by calling Jesus Emmanuel, which means "God is with us" (Matt. 1:23). Every day is Christmas for people who pray. Through prayer, they let God into their lives. Through prayer, they know, with the deepest knowing, that God cares for them and gives them light when they ask. Prayer is not the only spiritual-growth facilitator, but it is among the most powerful.

WHY PRAYER WORKS

In *The Christ of Every Road*, E. Stanley Jones, the great twentieth-century Christian writer and missionary, wrote that he found himself better or worse as he prayed more or less. "It works with almost mathematical precision," he said. Jones was merely reporting the results of Paul's advice to all disciples: "Let God remold your minds from within" (Rom. 12:2 Phillips). Spiritual growth occurs by letting God reinvent us, and we open the door for this to happen when we pray.

How, exactly, does prayer facilitate spiritual growth in us? Most human behavior patterns come from subconscious forces that originated during our childhood years. Behavior patterns therefore seldom change by logic alone. They change only when new information (a) gets past the defenses of the logical mind; (b) penetrates the subconscious; and (c) replaces the behavior shaper (feeling) which controls that particular thinking and acting habit. Prayer sets up the best possible physiological, psychological, and spiritual conditions for that to happen.

Physiological Conditions. The supplanting of old behavior shapers with new ones is far more likely to happen when alpha waves are the brain's predominant electrical activity (rather than the beta waves). The alpha mode presents the best opportunity for new information to move through the cerebral wall of rational defenses. Biofeedback machines used in the medical world tell us that this happens when we pray.

Psychological Conditions. Inventors like Edison understand that new ideas sometimes move into the conscious mind from the subconscious—usually following a period when the conscious mind has been thinking about that subject. Likewise, new ideas that reshape our behavior patterns can move down into the subconscious from the conscious mind—then resurface in conscious thinking and behavior at a later time.

Both experiences—ideas for new inventions and behavior shapers—are more likely to occur during a predominantly alpha wave mental state than at any other time. This happens best when (a) new information on this subject has repeatedly entered the consciousness; (b) the physical muscles and the mind are in a relaxed state; and (c) the mind's attention is directed somewhere other than that at which it usually points (a different place, idea, person, object). Prayer provides these circumstances.

Spiritual Conditions. Many people believe that the subconscious mind is connected to the mind of God (some call this cosmic intelligence). Whatever we call it, this connection is strongest (furnishes the best communication link) when we pray or meditate. God's Holy Spirit works through the subconscious. When the mind gives its attention to God through prayer, new information can get through the wall between the conscious and the subconscious mind.

Much evidence from parapsychological research at Duke University and elsewhere indicates that the subconscious mind is also connected in some way, a way that may be similar to radio waves, to the subconscious mind of all other human beings—perhaps through the mind of God.[1] Few other plausible explanations are available for mental telepathy—the ability of information to travel between two people across hundreds of miles, and even continents. This also provides the best presently available explanation for the reason praying for other people seems to help them. By prayer, it is possible that God communicates with their subconscious.

The subconscious never dies. This may be what Jesus meant when he spoke of eternal life. The immortality of the subconscious (which some call the soul) is irrelevant to the physical body. Under certain circumstances, the subconscious of living persons apparently seem to connect with the subconscious of persons already dead. This may account for the "Bridey Murphy" stories of the late 1950s, the ancient idea of reincarnation, and the more recent reports of New Age writers. What actually happens probably is a thought connection between two subconscious minds, one of which no longer resides on our plane of reality.

PRAYER POWER RESULTS

This old Moravian table prayer is often recited in unison: "Come, Lord Jesus, our guest to be, and bless these gifts given by thee. Bless our dear ones everywhere and keep them in your loving care. Amen." Prayer facilitates spiritual growth by making Christ a guest in our mind, through the power of the Holy Spirit. When that happens, we grow spiritually in many ways. Four of these ways are especially important.

First, we find a guidance system for life priorities that is wiser than our unaided rational thinking. Setting priorities is not enough unless they are the *right* priorities. Our most deadly danger is putting massive energy into climbing a ladder that leans against the wrong wall. Hard work is not the key to meaningful living; working hard at the right things is the key. Jesus warned the Pharisees against placing their ladders against a wall of religious rules. We easily see the false reality of those walls. Yet, we sometimes pick other walls that, although much different in appearance, are equally unreal. Prayer protects us from setting phony priorities and climbing toward an empty future.

Tim Hansel gave the following formula for successful living in his book *Eating Problems for Breakfast:*

1. Pray
2. Work
3. Pray
4. Work

In the frantic pace of living, we may forget that priceless principle. The worth of our life and efforts is not determined by our efforts, but by the directions in which those efforts point. Prayer helps us to set and maintain priorities that are worth arriving at.

Second, we find a strength greater than the strength of our willpower. A man fought an alcohol problem for twenty years. Most of the time, he lost. Six months into recovery, a friend asked him how he stayed dry now when he never could before.

He said, "I pray. That is the key to it. I never let a day go by without praying. I wish I had learned that a long time ago."

When the Holy Spirit enters the unconscious through the avenue of prayer, new power becomes available. Prayer can change our thinking and behavior in the same way reprogramming alters the course of activity in a computer. Prayer resets our inclinations closer to the image of God at the center of our being—moving us away from the unreality which we center on, intentionally or unintentionally, when we lose that focus.

When Peter jumped out of the boat and began walking toward Jesus on the water, he did fine for a while. Then he apparently lost his focus on Christ and began to concentrate on water-walking. As he sank into the waves, he prayed a short prayer of desperation: "Lord, save me!" Jesus reached out and caught him, bringing him back to the reality of God, rescuing him from the reality of self (Matt. 14:29-31). Countless people have similar life experiences. The psalmist said, "I call upon the Lord, who is worthy to be praised, so I shall be saved from my enemies" (Ps. 18:3). One of the enemies from which prayer saves us is ourselves. People who pray daily say that it keeps them more focused, thereby reducing the number of overwhelming circumstances into which they might fall.

Third, we find a new kind of love, more powerful than that which we can manufacture through good intentions. This is what St. Teresa of Avila meant when she said that the people who listen to God most will love others most: "They will love others much more than they did, with a more genuine love, with greater passion and with a love which brings more profit."[2]

People often ask, "How can I love someone who has done all these bad things to me?" The answer is that you cannot— not by yourself. By yourself, you are not strong enough or big enough or forgiving enough. But by asking God to love that someone through you with his power, you can. That was what Jesus meant when he said, "Love your enemies" (Matt. 5:44). He was not saying, "Do it yourself." He was saying, "Do it through and because of your powerful relationship with God." Love is not something we must work at. Love results from what we are on the inside, derived primarily from our relationship with God. This fruit of the Spirit of God inside us grows inadequately without a prayer connection with God.

Fourth, we find a feeling of joy that lifts us beyond our circumstances. A friend asked a man experiencing some turbulent business reverses how things were going.

"Just great!" he replied. "Business wasn't too good last week, but it will be better this week. I can do all things through Christ who strengthens me. If God is for me, who can be against me?" And he meant it. This man, who had lived much of his life in constant fear of the future, had discovered the joy of putting his trust somewhere other than in his circumstances.

Prayer begins when we open our mind's door from the inside. But our own initiative does not determine everything that happens in that transaction. When we pray, God often speaks to us and helps us in ways that we neither requested nor anticipated. Prayer is like the "enhanced" 911 system now in use in many American communities. When a call comes in, the person in trouble does not need to give name, address, and phone number. That information automatically appears on the operator's computer screen. "Draw near to God, and he will draw near to you," says James (4:8). That happens when we pray. God's enhanced 911 knows our location and needs. Thus God moves in our direction, filling in the gaps we cannot provide, giving us the answers and power that we lack the ability to request.

PRAYER CLASSES

After Jesus' disciples recognized the source of his power, they said, "Lord, teach us to pray" (Luke 11:1). Many contemporary disciples seek similar information: What kinds of prayer are effective in helping us to grow spiritually? The answers to that question fall into two general categories: individual prayer and congregational prayer.

Individual Prayer. Jesus prayed alone (Mark 1:35) and recommended it to others (Matt. 6:6). Unless we are willing to be alone with God, we have trouble hearing God above the traffic noise of circumstantial and cerebral distractions. Even though we could pray all the time, anywhere, that is unlikely to happen unless we decide to pray at a specific place at some specific time. God enters our presence best when we enter solitary silence.

Even when they set a time to be alone and undistracted, most people have difficulty opening a conversation with God. One pastor says that is because our minds are running at 10,000 RPM, but they must be at 500 RPM in order to hear God. That pastor, who uses a journal, begins by writing down what happened yesterday. That, he says, gets his mind down from 10,000 to 5,000. To get it on down to 500 RPM, he prays the ACTS formula: Adoration, Confession, Thanksgiving, Supplication. Then he listens.[3]

The Secret to Abundant Living: Learning How to Ask

"Ask, and it will be given you; search, and you will find; knock, and the door will be opened for you" (Matt. 7:7).
"In the morning, while it was still very dark, he got up and went out to a deserted place, and there he prayed" (Mark 1:35).

The following model, which has helped thousands of people to develop the ability to connect with God involves ten steps. (See the Resource Section for obtaining this formula on billfold-size cards.)

TEN STEPS TO GOD

Most people feel that they should pray, but few know how. The following steps, if used for fifteen minutes daily, will enable you to experience God's peace, joy, and power in a way you have never known before.

As you begin this adventure, remember that prayer is an experience, not an idea. In some ways, prayer is like riding a bicycle. You learn only by doing it, never by thinking about doing it.

Commit yourself to methodically following these ten steps for fourteen consecutive days. Most people report that they do not experience God's presence as fully during the first three or four days as after several days of practice. Persist in reaching out, and God will come to you. Like falling in love, the experience of God's presence is impossible to define. But when it happens, you will understand why great Christian leaders of every century have so enthusiastically recommended and practiced prayer. And you will understand what Jeremiah meant: "You will seek me and find me when you seek me with all your heart" (Jer. 29:13 NIV).

1. In preparation, set aside fifteen minutes in a location where you can be physically relaxed and there is little likelihood of interruption. Read one or two chapters from the Bible, listening for what God says to you. This helps to erase distracting thoughts from the blackboard of your mind. The following passages are especially helpful in preparing for prayer: John 14; Psalm 23; Matthew 5:1-12; Romans 8:35-39; I Corinthians 13; Psalm 91; Matthew 6; John 3:1-17; Psalm 46; Romans 12; John 15; Psalm 27; Psalm 103; Psalm 121; Isaiah 55; Luke 15; Psalm 84; John 1:1-18; Psalm 90; Psalm 19; I John 4:7-21; Psalm 139; Luke 24; Psalm 130; Luke 18:1-17.

2. Close your eyes and give thanks for three personal blessings of which you are especially conscious today. This helps you move toward God by moving away from a sense of your own self-sufficiency.

3. Ask God to help three other persons whom you feel need God's help today. Ask God to help your pastor(s). This helps you move toward God by moving away from self-centeredness.

4. Ask God to forgive your mistakes and sins, and give you the strength to forgive others.

5. Ask God to help one person you find it hard to like. Ask God to give that person insights into his/her personal problems, and ask for the power to let God's love flow through you to him/her.

6. Ask that you be sensitive today to the needs of one person with whom you can share God's love in word or deed.

7. Ask for insights into your personal problems.

8. Ask for help in achieving your personal goals.

9. Ask that God tell you the most important thing you need to do today in order to "seek first his kingdom" (Matt. 6:33*a* NIV).

10. Conclude by listening intently for three minutes to what God may say to you.[4]

Whatever pattern of prayer each individual finds spiritually helpful, his or her conversations with God are nourished by a growing recognition of the following principles:

1. Prayer often begins as a ritual or a discipline. Through experience, prayer grows into a joyful power.

2. Prayer is much more than a magical way of getting goodies from God. Through prayer, God tunes the instrument of our desires and wills to the pitch of God's wisdom.

3. God hears what we need to say, even when we cannot clearly articulate it—"the Spirit comes to the aid of our weakness" (Rom. 8:26 NEB).

4. Communicating with God involves listening as well as talking.

During the Rose Bowl Parade in Pasadena, California, a few years ago, a float stalled. Frustration gradually increased because the floats behind it could not move ahead. Mechanics crawled under the flower-covered vehicle and tinkered with the motor. Nothing happened. Eventually, they discovered the problem: no gas. As someone went for fuel, the crowd realized that the float's sponsor was one of the major oil companies! The power available to every Christian far exceeds fossil fuel, or even nuclear energy. This—the greatest force in the universe—begins to energize our living, when we (a) learn how to pray and (b) pray.

Congregational Prayer. When a nightclub opened on Main Street, the only church in a small town organized an all-night prayer meeting. The members asked God to burn down the club. Within a few minutes, lightning struck the club, and it burned to the ground. The owner sued the church, which denied responsibility.

After hearing both sides, the judge said, "It seems that wherever the guilt may lie, the tavern keeper is the one who really believes in prayer, while the church doesn't!"[5]

Evidence could easily be gathered for similar indictments against many congregations. Most churches highly recommend prayer. However, during a calendar year, the amount of time these churches spend teaching people how to pray would provide sufficient evidence to convict them of not believing in it. When the disciples prayed together for Peter's release from prison, "the place in which they were gathered together was shaken" (Acts 4:31). When contemporary disciples do not emphasize God's leadership through corporate prayer, their group settles into a routine that its members begin to feel is predominantly social rather than spiritual.

Leaders of churches that develop a strong prayer emphasis say that the following factors are especially important.

1. The pastor is highly committed to practicing and preaching prayer.

2. The church develops prayer ministries as intentionally as it organizes Sunday school and other church programs.

3. The leaders provide training in prayer through annual events and incorporation into various ongoing programs.[6]

Numerous programs compete for attention in church life. Leaders must keep committees operational, run the Christian education program, and do countless other important chores. In that flurry of activity, helping people learn how to relate to God in prayer is easily displaced with "more practical matters." Most congregations therefore lack any type of organized prayer program. The Wednesday-night prayer meeting disappeared from mainline congregational life during the 1940s and 1950s. Most churches replaced it with generalized preachments about the importance of prayer, but not with models that offer opportunities for participation. This vacuum explains why church members respond so positively to the various types of prayer-chain models in contemporary use. (The Resource Section contains information for obtaining several of the systems available for involving the entire congregation.)

Congregational prayer programs can help to change the statistics described by George Gallup: "In a typical day the average person stays in front of the TV set nearly twenty-five times longer than in prayer. We say we are believers, but perhaps we are only *assenters*."[7] Unless congregations give the teaching of prayer intentional attention, they can fall into the situation described by a popular Texas newspaper columnist:

> An insurance man who also owned some farm acreage said that all the cotton in his county had been wiped out by hail.
> A friend said, "Your crop was insured, of course."
> "Well, no," the insurance man answered sheepishly.
> "Your neighbors' crops weren't insured, either?" the friend asked.
> "Most of them were."
> Playing a hunch, the friend asked, "Who'd they get their insurance from?"
> "Me," the insurance agent said miserably."[8]

Some people do not pray because they do not know how. That can happen to large numbers of people when congregations that recommend prayer take little or none of it for themselves.

THE INVISIBLE KEY

Strong evidence indicates that prayer can power both individual spiritual growth and congregational vitality:

- Champion Forest Baptist Church of Houston, Texas, grew from 500 members in 1978 to 2,800 in 1990. The pastor explained the growth by saying that "prayer undergirds everything. When we work, *we* work, but when we pray, *God* works!"

- Central Community Church of Wichita, Kansas, has nearly doubled in size during the last five years. That, the staff explains, can be accounted for only through prayer.[9]

Like the food supply for an army, prayer simultaneously feeds the individual Christian's spiritual growth and the church's effectiveness in its mission. If prayer is not emphasized, both starve.

A cartoon showed a huge crowd gathered in front of a church, under the spreading branches of a large tree. The pastor is standing on the church steps in a black robe.

He says, "Have I ever told you the parable of the man who left his keys at home?"[10]

Some aspects of church life are important; others are essential. Prayer is one of the essential aspects. Without that emphasis in making and maintaining a God connection, church leaders lock many people out of spiritual growth. Unlocking those doors does not guarantee that everyone will enter, but it greatly increases the possibility.

Chapter 6

THE PEOPLE
CONNECTION

E very summer, 2,500 young people come to Estes Park, Colorado, for the National Youth Congress. Each year, the leaders conduct a poll to identify the major personal concerns of youth. Two needs always stand at the top of the list: (a) to get closer to God; and (b) to love and to be loved.[1] Surveys among adults reveal the same desires. People want spiritual growth, and they want caring relationships with others. When Jesus defined spiritual maturity as loving God and loving people (Mark 12:30-31), he was also prescribing the answer to basic human needs.

Most clergy characterize the relationship between those two aspects of spiritual maturity—loving God and loving people—like this: Strengthening our connection with God strengthens our ability to love our neighbors. Far fewer pastors recognize the potential power in the opposite equation: *Strengthening our emotional connection with people can (under the right circumstances) strengthen our spiritual connection with God.* The survey evidence that forms a backdrop for this book strongly suggests (a) the validity of that latter equation; and (b) most pastors tend to underemphasize the truth in one of Jesus' most familiar statements: "Where two or three are gathered in my name, I am there among them" (Matt. 18:20).

Laypeople seem to see Jesus' insight more clearly than do clergy: The laity ranked fellowship number three on the list of factors that have helped them grow spiritually; clergy ranked fellowship seven. For pastors, the top seven spiritual growth facilitators were, in order of importance in their personal lives: worship, Bible study, prayer, preaching, retreats, service, and *fellowship*. Laypersons ranked the most helpful spiritual growth facilitators quite differently: worship, prayer, *fellowship*, preaching, service, Bible study, and stewardship.

This explains why pastors tend to underemphasize the role of fellowship in facilitating spiritual growth. They, of course, give leadership to churches out of their own personal spiritual growth experience, rather than from a lay perspective.

Pastors are therefore likely to say, as one pastor did, "I feel that Bible study to know what God wants for us in our lives is most important—fellowship and service will follow." Most laypersons' opinions contrast sharply with that view. They are more likely to say something like one of these statements, selected from a list of similar observations:

- "Fellowship is #1."
- "Fellowship, phone calls, and communication with other Christians is the key element."
- "The fellowship of the congregation and clergy strengthens me more than anything else."
- "The love, dedication, and commitment which I saw in my peers was something I wanted in my life. It was more than 'fellowship' or a cookie hour—it was real—it was family. It turned my life around."

Other research has verified the importance of fellowship in facilitating spiritual growth. George Gallup notes that many respondents in his survey credited their relationship with other people as a decisive element in their faith growth.[2] Sociologist George Barna says that people who do not participate beyond worship in the activities of their church find that worship alone tends not to provide a substantial benefit for their lives.[3]

Paul's suggestion to the Hebrews is much more than a handy motivator for church attendance in the doldrums of summer: "Let us consider how to provoke one another to love and good deeds, not neglecting to meet together, as is the habit of some, but encouraging one another" (10:24-25). Paul was speaking to the essential role of "people connectedness" in maintaining and strengthening our spiritual connection with God. John says, "If we walk in the light as he himself is in the light, we have fellowship with one another" (I John 1:7). That fellowship, in turn, provides more spiritual light for the road toward God.

BEYOND SOLITARY CONFINEMENT

The value of fellowship for strengthening spiritual growth is even greater in contemporary America, where loneliness is now unparalleled since frontier days. In this country of wanderers, more than 17 percent change their place of residence each year. Many people relate more to electronic gadgets than to one another. Entertainment centers were once associated with people; now they contain furniture and equipment. The consequences of this human unconnectedness are tragic: Record suicide levels and a society of loners, many of whom yearn for relationships, but scarcely know how to perfect them when the opportunities arise.

Author C. S. Lewis was accurate when he noted that people are not sufficient for their own bliss.[4] The prevalence of youth gangs illustrates the lengths to which many people will go to alleviate their sense of disconnectedness. Joining a gang prevents the cold ice of solitary confinement from seeping into the pores of the soul. Adults will go to similar extremes in their attempts to alleviate the pain of loneliness. This is one of the reasons the Seventh Day Adventists, Jehovah's Witnesses, and Mormons are growing as religious groups. They have developed skills in loving lonely people—giving them the sense of connectedness (fellowship) they lack. People respond to these healing relationships by opening themselves to a closer connection with God.

Other denominations could undoubtedly do equally well in providing fellowship as a spiritual-growth facilitator—if they more clearly recognized the need. Many mainline clergy, however, apparently are blocked from the necessary perceptions. Because fellowship has not been a major factor in their personal spiritual development, they do not see its importance.

Not all mainline leaders, however, fail to see this need. Some pastors are recognizing the necessity for fellowship as an element in the spiritual growth of members. Bruce Larson—long recognized for his contribution to the field of relational theology—is now co-pastor of The Crystal Cathedral at Garden Grove, California. This 10,000-member congregation has more than 300 small groups meeting each month. Larson writes:

> I don't believe you can have a live church without a significant number of your members in small groups. It is out of the small groups that God's healing takes place, as well as the equipping and deploying of people in lay ministry—which is the bottom line of the church.
>
> This is where people learn ministry and learn how to be channels of healing and help and encouragement and affirmation and correction to others, as well as hearing their call to become involved in the structures of society and in the evangelizing of their neighbors. It's where ministry is implemented and encouraged and where wounds are healed as a result.[5]

The word *fellowship* is formed by linking *fellow* (which means people) with *ship*. *Fellowship* means people traveling together in the same ship. Most people need that feeling. They do not enjoy traveling the sea of life in a one-person rowboat. Church leaders whose congregations are most effective at enhancing spiritual growth grasp this truth and build spiritual oceanliners.

After Jesus was crucified, two disciples on their way to Emmaus were talking about what had happened. "While they were walking and discussing, Jesus himself came near and went with them" (Luke 24:15). Since that day, many other disciples have had similar experiences. When they are together, the mind of Christ often joins them. The more they are together, the more Christ's mind continues to energize their lives—long after the meeting is over. As churches increasingly recognize the spiritual power of fellowship, they will place greater emphasis on the organizational processes needed to accomplish it.

A THREE-LANE HIGHWAY

Fellowship happens in three kinds of church groups: (1) those that focus on loving; (2) those that focus on learning; and (3) those that focus on doing. In some churches, traffic is heavy on all three lanes; in other churches, traffic flows in only one or two of the lanes. Congregations seem most effective when all three lanes are open.

The degree to which spiritual growth happens through these three types of groups in a particular congregation depends upon several factors: (a) whether the church provides all three kinds of groups; (b) whether the type of groups provided within each of the three categories matches the needs of people in every adult age bracket in the congregation; (c) the quality of each group's leadership; (d) the quality of each group's interpersonal relationship atmosphere; (e) the percentage of active church members involved in the groups; (f) the congregation's written or unwritten expectations regarding whether members should be involved in a group of some type; (g) the effectiveness of the church's system for drawing new and present members into the groups; and (h) how hard the clergy and lay leaders work at getting church members involved in the various types of groups. If several of these factors are missing, the number of people who report spiritual growth through group participation stays small. If most of these factors are present, many people find their spiritual growth enhanced through group participation.

Despite the obvious complexity required for developing and leading groups, churches have been relatively effective in that endeavor. A Gallup survey indicates that 28 percent of Americans are involved in a church group. Of the attenders, 74 percent say that these groups helped them "feel closer to God." The groups are so well respected that another 10 percent of Americans say they would like to become involved in one.[6] A review of the three primary types of spiritual-growth facilitating groups can help us see why people hold them in high esteem.

Loving Groups. The exploding number of self-help groups are among the most obvious illustrations in this category. More than 155 different types of 12-step groups are now operating—from AA (Alcoholics Anonymous) to divorce-recovery groups to drug-related groups. While these groups often are interdenominational or based in a secular setting, many of them meet in church buildings. Increasingly, churches actually sponsor the groups, and some authorities recommend that 60 percent of a church's groups be of this type.

The spiritual dimension of these groups is not highly advertised, but attenders report spirituality as a strong undercurrent. Some attenders make the group a substitute for church (a few AA members attend as many as four meetings a week). However, most group members report spiritual growth that strengthens their church connections. Many attenders make comments such as the following: "The twelve-step program in OA (Overeaters Anonymous) has brought me closer to God and to this church."

These groups are especially popular among Baby Boomers returning to church after one or two decades of self-imposed exile. Searching for meaning with the "What's in it for me?" attitude common to this age bracket, they go where their needs are met. Many describe their quest as "spiritual" rather than "religious," although it often brings them home to the church. The traffic of young adults on this lane of the fellowship highway is so heavy that some authorities see self-help groups as the best form of contemporary evangelism. The church's caring becomes a magnet that draws people to its sanctuaries through side doors.

Among the other church groups that fall into the "focus on loving" category, seniors' groups are especially valuable. An Arizona church, whose membership consists almost exclusively of retirees, provides twenty Friendship Circles. Each year the membership is divided into these twenty groups. They carefully put one to three strong extroverts in each group, mixing in singles and persons who are not yet church members. In a Philadelphia congregation, the seniors' program averages more than sixty persons at each monthly meeting, and its group tours are transported on its own bus. The casual observer may classify these as social groups. Participants know that they can be much more. The transactions are predominantly social, but many of the results are spiritual.

Among other groups that fall into this "focus on loving" category are singles groups, youth groups, and widows groups. Every human being needs a sense of belonging, self-esteem, an opportunity to express love, and a chance to feel loved. Church groups that meet those needs often also facilitate spiritual growth. (See the Resource Section for blueprints for seniors groups and young-adult fellowship/social groups.)

Learning Groups. The traditional adult Sunday school class is the most obvious example in this category. Participation in an adult class strengthens the spiritual health of both the participants and the congregation in at least five ways:

1. It provides a sense of family through the social and psychological nurturing relationships of a small, caring group.

2. It increases the growth in spiritual maturity that helps people to enrich their personal lives through absorbing Christian thinking and behavior principles.

3. It increases the percentage of church members who exhibit active Christian discipleship in and beyond the congregation.

4. It provides an effective way to enfold new members into the church family through their involvement in a warm, accepting social group.

5. It provides the small-group "bonding" that decreases the likelihood of church members drifting out the back door to inactivity during periods of congregational unrest.

For various reasons, however, many congregations fail to take full advantage of the spiritual-growth facilitating potential in adult Sunday school classes:

• Some leaders feel that adult Sunday church school classes are as old-fashioned as buggy whips. Even some Christian-education "experts" fail to see their significance.

• Congregations in some denominations are afflicted with the "confirmation syndrome." Becoming a confirmed member is a lengthy (and sometimes boring) process. Teenagers learn that completing confirmation class means never needing to study the Bible again. (Some also learn that they never want to do so again!)

• Some church leaders fail to recognize that the way American adults relate to groups has changed—due partially to educational levels far higher than those of previous generations. Churches now need more adult classes. Contemporary adult classes seldom exceed 35 persons on the roll, with an average attendance of 20. Adults of this generation want to discuss the lesson rather than merely listen to lectures. Therefore, when a class grows beyond 20, many of its members are unable to talk and thus have less interest in attending. Unawareness of this "35/20 phenomenon" sometimes keeps leaders from seeing the need to organize new classes as the church membership grows.

• Some church leaders are blocked from establishing new classes because members of present classes protest that they would like to have new church members in their class.

Sincere in their convictions, they do not realize that many more persons will join a new class than one that was established years ago.

- Some large churches fail to note that they can occasionally form a new adult class from one of their four-week Sunday-morning "Information Classes" for prospective new members.

- Some churches lack sufficient rooms in their building to house a new class.

Existing adult classes more often malfunction at the organizational structure and social-extroversion levels than because of content deficiencies. To increase effectiveness in both areas, each class, from the beginning of its existence, should form a leadership structure that involves: (a) a teacher; (b) a membership-care coordinator; (c) a social-activities coordinator, whose job is to organize a monthly social activity; (d) a hospitality coordinator, whose job is to make first-time visitors and new attenders feel socially comfortable in the group; and (e) a "recruitment coordinator," who is responsible for attracting and involving new attenders. These five persons should serve on a "leadership team" within each class and focus on involving the class members in the behavior implicit in their titles. Such a procedure counterbalances the inclination of the quality and attendance of adult classes to rise or fall on the energy level of the teacher.

Four ingredients are particularly significant for increasing adult class extroversion:

1. *A gregarious leader.* Always early, he or she remembers names and faces and has a social knack for making strangers feel like home folks.

2. *Name tags every Sunday, for every class attender.* This makes newcomers feel equal to the regular attenders and reduces the social awkwardness of feeling that everyone is acquainted except you.

3. *Coffee, tea, and munchies in each classroom.* The coffeepot distributes more than caffeine. Everyone knows how to fix and

drink a cup of coffee. This gives strangers something specific to do with their hands.

4. *Monthly class social events.* Invitations to picnics and parties are much more personal than invitations to attend a Sunday school class. Hence, they increase the feeling of acceptance.

All large churches, and many mid-size churches, should start one new adult class each year. Yet, building space limitations and a shortage of how-to information often stifle that process. (See the Resource Section for ways to address both problems.) Regardless of what methods are used, however, leaders must remember that starting new classes is an inexact science. Approximately 60 percent of new classes blossom into permanent ones. For reasons beyond anyone's control, the others will wither and eventually disappear.

This failure percentage should not dissuade leaders from launching new classes. Instead, they must forge ahead courageously, while recognizing that they never have total control of this process. No matter how great their wisdom or how excellent their methods, leaders cannot actually create new classes; they can only set up the circumstances in which new classes can invent themselves.

During the last two decades, a cousin of the adult Sunday school class has emerged in various formats. Meeting at a time other than Sunday morning, these groups are variously named; Bible study, covenant groups, discussion groups, support groups, and growth groups are among the most popular labels. The most notable examples of success in terms of a high percentage of the congregation being involved in these groups come from the evangelical side of the denominational spectrum. Importing and adopting the small-group pattern from Korean churches, some Assembly of God congregations have succeeded in involving 60 percent of their members in weekly groups that focus on prayer, study, sharing, caring, and evangelistic outreach. In one Missouri Synod Lutheran church, whose membership is more than 1,000, almost everyone is in a small group of some kind. Forty-three Bible-study groups meet weekly.

George Gallup says that developing such groups should be a top agenda item for all churches—he recommends that the groups focus on Bible study, teaching people to pray, and learning the ways of Christian faith from one another.[7] The following comments from parishioners who were asked what helped them grow spiritually provide strong evidence that Gallup is right:

- "The *most* influential element in my spiritual growth has been a series of small-group 'cell' type of experiences of an ongoing nature, in which I have been both a participant and a leader."
- "A group that includes a combination of prayer, Bible study, fellowship, and encouragement."
- "The group gave me a sense of community and belonging— five couples, close friends, intimates, fellow seekers."
- "Specific studies in small groups on spirituality and spiritual discipline."
- "Small group prayer, praise, study."

The challenge: Will mainline congregations gain the ability to involve people in such groups? Despite all the talk about small groups among mainline pastors, not many congregations are actually doing what they frequently discuss. Few mainline congregations succeed at involving more than 20 percent of their members in such groups. Various types of materials and resources for these groups are abundantly available. What seems lacking is: (a) the motivation of pastors to organize them; (b) the receptivity to small-group attendance among the types of persons who choose to attend a mainline church; and especially, (c) a small-group model that has proved itself in a mainline church, one from which other churches can learn—one that actually involves more than 50 percent of church members in weekly groups. With all the current interest in this matter, a breakthrough method will surely appear in the next few years.

Doing Groups. The most abundant existing example of this type of group is the least effective with regard to facilitating spiritual growth: committees. Most people who join churches want to help accomplish worthwhile goals, but only a small percentage want to serve on committees. That position seems justified. In the study that formed a basis for this book, *not a single opinion-poll respondent indicated that committee service provided spiritual growth!*

"Doing" groups that do sometimes succeed in facilitating spiritual growth include women's groups; men's groups; mission-project teams; care teams that visit the ill, bereaved, and troubled; and food-kitchen volunteers. Many groups of this type are multicongregational or multidenominational. The Evangelical Lutheran Church in America, for example, has a "Mission Builders Program." Volunteers, most of whom are retired, spend several months each year constructing new church buildings. These people report that significant spiritual growth results from their experiences. An example of a multidenominational "doing group" is the Habitat for Humanity program.

How can church leaders begin to enlarge spiritual-growth opportunities through loving, learning, and doing groups?

Ask the appropriate committee to review the membership list and put a check mark by the names of individuals who are actively involved in a loving, learning, or doing group (do not include committee membership). What percentage of the members are *not* involved in such a group? Generally speaking, people are likely to decide to become involved in such a group either: (a) when they are invited to lead or help form a new group; or (b) when they are invited to lead or help form a new activity, project, or study within an established group. At least one instance of both of these opportunities should occur every year in every church.

Set a goal of establishing three new groups during each of the next five years—groups that will focus on one or more of these three spiritual-growth facilitating qualities: loving, learning, and doing.

GETTING AWAY FROM IT ALL

One type of fellowship is so powerful that it deserves special attention: *retreats*. This is one of the points, however, at which pastors and laity report quite different experiences. Pastors rank retreats as number five on their list of spiritual-growth facilitators. Laypeople report retreats as number ten. Most of the difference in perspective can undoubtedly be explained by the large number of opportunities most clergy have for retreat experiences—defined here as any opportunity to leave daily life for a time of reflection, study, prayer, learning, and/or discussion. Ninety percent of pastors attend some sort of professionally oriented retreat each year, and many serve as youth retreat leaders. This undoubtedly explains why so many pastors comment in the following ways:

- "As a pastor, I believe retreats to be number one."
- "Retreats—the most beneficial to my spiritual growth."
- "Retreats—very important to me at critical points in my life."
- "National conferences/gatherings which include good preaching and study."

By contrast, many of the laypeople who reported spiritual-growth experiences through retreats were referring to a different type of retreat. The site was sometimes local, such as a church-sponsored Lay Witness Mission. Pastors might not classify those local weekend renewal events as "retreats." However, for many laypeople, they provide a chance to draw apart from the daily routine and examine life's directions and values from a new perspective.

One layperson said that after a Lay Witness weekend, he joined a small group. "We learned and had fellowship. Jesus Christ came into my life, and God's Holy Spirit changed me."

While relatively few laypeople have the opportunity to attend a retreat away from their local community, those people often report that spiritual growth resulted from that experience. Weekend retreats—such as those originated by the Roman Catholic Church and several mainline denominations—are frequently cited as positive spiritual-growth experiences. After the three-day "Walk to Emmaus," a layman wrote:

> During the communion service at the Walk, I felt God's love, his grace, and his mercy come over me, changing my life. When the service was over, I had lost all my hate, bitterness, and unforgiveness. People can see the difference in me, and I praise God that I can feel the difference he has made in me. The Emmaus Walk is one reason I think we have seen growth in our church over the past year or so.[8]

Why are retreats (whether local or out of town) often such powerful change agents? People experience the same spiritual-growth facilitators as in other fellowship settings, but in a far more concentrated way. Then too, following many of these retreats, the attenders form small groups that meet weekly to reflect upon their spiritual lives. The fellowship begun at the retreat deepens and strengthens the attenders' faith as it intertwines with prayer and Bible study over the next several months. (See the Resource Section for several types of spiritual-growth retreats.)

Jesus experienced the God-given power for direction that sometimes comes from retreats. Luke reports far more instances of Jesus praying than do the other three Gospel writers. In many cases, those prayers took place in a retreat setting. If Jesus needed to retreat in order to deepen his God connection, how much more do his present-day disciples need that experience?

ACTION PRESCRIPTION

The average Christian sees fellowship as a more powerful source of spiritual growth than Bible study. This data should inform our church life in at least four ways:

1. Involve as many people as possible in one of the three types of fellowship groups—loving, learning, and doing. That helps to overcome the charge that we go to football games to do our shouting, to the movies to do our crying, and to church to do our freezing.

2. Send clergy to out-of-town seminars designed specifically to facilitate personal spiritual growth. Leaders cannot effectively give away what they do not have.

3. Encourage as many laypeople as possible to attend high-quality out-of-town spiritual-growth retreats.

4. Find ways to organize local multicongregational, multidenominational retreats, using qualified outside leadership that is acceptable to all the churches. Only a minute percentage of laypeople can attend retreats at distant sites. Bring the retreats to them.

Fellowship is at the heart of followership—and often produces more of it. Jesus said to the disciples, "I have called you friends" (John 15:15). (He did not say, "I have taught you how to study the Old Testament.") When we set up systems and circumstances in which we can treat people like genuine friends, the same thing often happens. They become stronger disciples, growing spiritually in ways that Bible study alone can never accomplish.

A line in Robert Fulghum's *All I Ever Really Needed to Know I Learned in Kindergarten* gives this advice: "When you go out into the world, watch for traffic . . . and stick together." The evidence indicates that Fulghum's advice is equally appropriate for disciples of Jesus Christ.

Chapter 7

TURNING ON
THE LIGHTS

T he boy attending church with his family was not expect-
ing anything important to happen. However, as the
sermon progressed, *something did happen!* New doors
opened in his mind. A powerful sense of direction formed.
Fifty years later, Harry Emerson Fosdick, one of the twentieth
century's most influential Christian thinkers, said that he
never escaped the influence of that hour. Countless other
people have had similar experiences. Preaching is often much
more than twenty minutes of rest, reverie, or reflection. Occasionally, it changes lives dramatically. Always, its potential
for influence far exceeds its tiny percentage of each week's
10,080 minutes.

*For the average layperson, preaching ranks above Bible study as a
spiritual-growth influence.* Commenting on the survey list of
twelve potential ways people can grow spiritually, one man
said, "I get more out of preaching than all the others com-
bined." Church history and contemporary observations help
us to see the basis for such comments. While small groups and
Bible study are powerful influences, they appeal to and touch
far fewer persons than does preaching.

When deepened spirituality appeared in Wesley's time,
Luther's time, and Jesus' time, preaching built the bridge. In
many historical eras of spiritual renewal, of course, the average person could not read. Thus, preaching was the only

option for obtaining biblical truth. In more recent times, most people can read, but few do. So the primary way the Bible's truth gets to the human mind is still through the spoken word. Someone must build a bridge between God and people, and many of the girders are words in sermons.

Americans, always the activists, tend to bad-mouth preaching. Phrases like "mere words" and "we need action, not words," express disdain for sermonizing. Yet, those cynical observations cannot survive careful scrutiny. Several kinds of evidence support an opposite conclusion regarding the power of words.

WORD POWER

Forty-two percent of Americans gather each weekend to hear words from the person in the pulpit. Why? They know that preaching offers greater likelihood of positive change than they can obtain through any other group or process available. In what other situation are we influenced to examine our deepest values and consider constructive change in our attitudes, behavior, and society? People gather for preaching because they know that "The most powerful stimulus for changing minds is not a chemical. Or a baseball bat. It is a word."[1]

The primary objective of preaching is to encourage spiritual maturity, defined in this manner: "Let the same mind be in you that was in Christ" (Phil. 2:5). According to Jesus' long-form definition of spiritual maturity, "You shall love the Lord your God with all your heart, and with all your soul, and with all your strength, and with all your mind; and your neighbor as yourself" (Luke 10:27). Jesus' short-form definition of spiritual maturity was: "Follow me" (Matt. 4:19). Spiritual *growth* means that we move in his direction. Spiritual *maturity* means we have arrived there. Preaching is not the only vehicle that can transport us toward that destination, but it is high on the list of the most useful.

Among its many implications, a spiritual maturity similar to that of Christ surely involves: (a) praying and thinking like Christ; (b) loving and feeling like Christ; and (c) talking and acting like Christ. Preaching encourages the traffic of our human inclinations to move in those directions. Thus, the New Testament puts preaching on a high pedestal:

- "Faith comes from what is heard, and what is heard comes by the preaching of Christ," Paul writes to the church at Rome (10:17 RSV).
- "For Christ did not send me to baptize but to preach," Paul writes to another church (I Cor. 1:17 RSV).
- Paul places preaching at the top of his list of spiritual gifts (I Cor. 12:28, 14:1).
- Paul says that love is the first aim of ministry, but he puts preaching second on the list (I Cor. 12, 13, 14).

Preaching is much more than "mere words." Preaching changes people for God and good. When Moses encountered God at the burning bush, he took off his sandals because he was standing on holy ground. Men customarily take off their hats when they enter church sanctuaries. In some traditions, women cover their heads. Perhaps both should remove their shoes instead. Anywhere the bridges to God are built with words is holy ground.

EMPTYING OUR CUP

A story is told about an American professor who went for instruction to a Japanese Zen master. The professor interrupted with a string of questions each time the master tried to explain something. Finally, the Zen master poured the professor some tea. When the teacup was full, the master kept pouring until the teapot emptied itself into the overflowing cup.

When the professor protested, the Zen master replied, "You are like this cup. You are so filled with your own knowledge, I cannot teach you anything."[2]

The average person, like that professor, is preoccupied with his or her own life experiences and perceptions. One of the major values of listening to a sermon is the pause it produces in our stream of consciousness. By stopping to listen, we acknowledge our need to replace our knowledge with God's knowledge.

A seminary preaching professor visited a small country church on vacation. The sermon, given by a retired preacher who had been asked to fill in for the vacationing pastor, was snail-paced and boring. Yet, at one point near the end, the visiting homiletics professor received a powerful personal insight. The spiritual growth that preaching can produce does not depend totally upon the speaker's eloquence. Even from the poorest preaching, listeners often gain spiritually helpful insights. This occurs because something more than preaching is happening when we listen to a sermon. That something is "attention." The worship service, particularly the preaching, provides an organized span of time in which people give attention to God. Thus, they sometimes receive life-changing insights, even when other parts of the sermon are rather dull.

This, of course, is why the Quakers find spiritual power in silence—with no spoken words whatever. The organized silence creates a block of time in which people give their attention to God. When we hold out the cup of our minds to God for a few minutes—whether in a high-quality sermon, a dull sermon, or just plain silence—it never comes away empty. We are spiritually nurtured. Coleridge said, "Faith is an affirmation and an act / That bids eternal truth be present fact."[3] Eternal truth cannot become present fact for us until we pay attention. Preaching helps that happen by providing the empty space in our consciousness that allows God-consciousness to enter.

Socrates said that an unexamined life is not worth living. The opposite extreme is also true. Many over-psychologized Americans suffer from the malady of continual self-analysis. Gazing too long and too compulsively at our interior state and feelings fills the horizon with self. In this illness, the only road to recovery is to focus the mind on God. That is what preaching helps us to do—regardless of the sermon's subject. Concentrating on the snarl of self and circumstances does not always solve our problems. Sometimes, turning our eyes away from the tangled yarn lets God undo it for us. Paying attention to preaching can let that happen.

WHAT KIND OF PREACHING?

Great preaching offers hope and help. These two ingredients move across the word-bridge from pulpit to pew, to the degree that each listener feels that the message relates to his or her daily life. That happens best and most frequently when the sermon contains insights that demonstrate the life-changing power of biblical truth.

Billy Graham's slogan in early years was "Anchored to the rock. Geared to the times." In 1946, he commented that most ministers were neither. Graham has become less critical of his colleagues since those days, but his observation still has merit. When a sermon fails to connect with the Bible and/or with contemporary human needs and issues, it fails.

Baby Boomers are especially inclined to judge a sermon's value by its biblical connections. Therefore, today's effective preaching construction is far more likely to fall into the classification of "expository," giving it obvious biblical rootage. "Topical" sermon construction communicated well with the 1950s young adults. Though many such sermons were solidly based on biblical truth, listeners four decades later often label that type of sermon superficial. Thus, sermons in sanctuaries packed with young adults often sound like Sunday school lessons, since they contain a high percentage of "teaching" elements. The strongest criticism contemporary young adults can throw at a sermon is not that it lacks eloquence, but that it lacks biblical foundations.

One person put it this way: "Preaching here is rarely spiritual or biblically based. The spiritual needs of our membership are expected to be served from the many fine activities or works of the church. Spiritual, biblical preaching would be a welcome addition to our church life."

In connecting with the Bible, today's effective sermon is more likely to focus on one central biblical truth, rather than unrolling a "drifting exposition" of a text or a series of verses. However the sermon is constructed, today's young adults expect its central point to grow out of the biblical text itself. A profound philosophical point that throws in a biblical text to give it religious flavor is not enough. For this generation, great preaching involves more than illuminating the truth about life. Great preaching is a matter of using light from the Bible to illuminate the truth about life.

A biblical basis alone is not enough, however. The sermon must speak to contemporary needs in a contemporary way. Effective sermon illustrations in this decade are therefore more likely to come from personal experiences, TV shows, movies, and current news stories, rather than from books or historical examples. This keeps the sermon sounding fresh and alive—and assures the congregation that the pastor is alive to the present time, as well as to the Bible's authority base.

In driving their truckload of hope and help across the word-bridge between pulpit and pew, contemporary pastors face new highway conditions created by television. Previous clergy communicated with a print-media generation. Today's crowd was raised on a mental diet of pictures. They can read, but pictures are the communication medium with which they are most comfortable. When they look toward the front of the sanctuary, the dials of their mental receivers are set on "visual"—not on "auditory" (like the radio generation) or on "conceptual" (like the print generation).

Effective contemporary preachers must therefore speak in a picture content that far exceeds that of their predecessors. Otherwise, their truckload of hope and help stalls on the bridge between pulpit and pew. This kind of talking-pictures preaching involves: (a) learning to marry biblical truth to human emotion; and (b) transmitting it through word pictures that pull the listener into the sermon and pull the Bible into the listener. Few pastors seem born with the skill for preaching to this TV generation. Most must learn it.

One pastor's seven-year-old daughter crawled into his chair one evening as he was reading a homiletics textbook.

"What kind of book is that?" she asked.

"It is a book about preaching," he replied.

"Oh, my," she said, her favorite expression at that time.

"Do you think that would be a good book to read?" he asked. When she unexpectedly said yes, he asked why.

"So I wouldn't have to listen to yours." Then she added, "Of course, I mostly don't listen to them anyway, just the jokes and the stories."

Her candid answer sums up what effective preaching must accomplish in order to gain admittance to the mind. The sermon must make interesting listening—involving the mind through images, stories, and illustrations. Otherwise, people would rather not "have to listen to yours."

The next-to-the-driest place on earth is the Atacama Desert in Chile, where no measurable rainfall has been reported for years. The driest place is at 11:00 A.M. on Sunday morning—in sermons that are poorly illustrated. An old story tells about some sailors who had just returned from a whaling voyage. While in port, they attended a local church service.

As they were leaving the building, one of the seamen said to the others, "It was a good sermon, but the skipper didn't have any harpoons on board." Before it can get results, preaching must get attention. Illustrations are the harpoons that pull the mind toward a connection with biblical truth. What is not heard cannot be absorbed.

The effective use of illustrations is not, of course, a result of doing what many beginners do—collect a string of illustrations and sermonize on the illustrations. That is preaching backward, making the sermon into an after-dinner speech—like "dividing the truth" with a rubber hammer instead of a two-edged sword. Illustrations should illustrate the point, not substitute for the point. But without illustrations, few people will get the point.

Churches increasingly use drama to draw people into the sermon's truth. The Willow Creek Community Church, northwest of Chicago, often uses a brief skit prior to the sermon, which then puts muscle on the biblical truth after the drama has drawn people into it. Other churches increasingly experiment in this direction. Drama cannot replace preaching, which communicates God through the powerful medium of a convinced personality. But drama is an excellent technique to involve people who grew up on more than thirty hours of TV per week. (See the Resource Section for obtaining Willow Creek dramas.)

Someone said that good teaching is one-fourth preparation and three-fourths theater. Preaching is more like that than we had thought. Studies have shown that 55 percent of a speaker's audience-impact is visual (how the speaker looks and acts). Another 38 percent of the speaker's impact is vocal (voice qualities such as pitch, resonance, volume, sincerity). Only 7 percent of the speaker's impact is verbal (content).[4] Thus, preaching preparation that focuses on communicating content alone seldom succeeds. How we come across is just as important as what we send across—especially if it blocks what we send across.

These factors are part of the reason some pastors have moved out of the pulpit to speak in a freestanding way. They are communicating in a manner that feels more contemporary to their audiences, especially the younger TV generation.

Moving away from the pulpit is not, however, mandatory for contemporary sermonizing—TV newscasters, after all, are seen only from the chest up. But contemporary preaching does require the preparation of communication, rather than the preparation of manuscripts. Sermons must be delivered live, rather than sounding as if they are from a "paper tape." (See the Resource Section for two helpful sermon preparation/delivery tools.)

Wise preachers try to find out how they are coming across. A pastor, wanting to obtain helpful feedback to strengthen his preaching, conducted this survey on Sunday morning:

> 1. Do I preach too long? ____yes ____no
> 2. Do my sermons help you? ____ never ____ sometimes ____ often ____ always
> 3. How can I do a better job of preaching?

All responses to the first question were "yes." In response to the second question, about 10 percent said "always," 10 percent said "never," 60 percent said "sometimes," and 20 percent said "often."[5] Such a poll does not tell the preacher everything, but it provides a place to start.

Effective preaching does not, however, depend only upon such elements, either alone or together. Preaching is effective when a mind's attention, focused on the message of the messenger, is moved by God's Spirit toward new life. Whether that happens depends also upon each listener's emotional, mental, and spiritual receptivity.

Through what a majority of listeners agreed was a dull, boring sermon, a certain man was converted to Christ.

"What caused you to make that decision?" the pastor asked him later.

The man answered, "It was when you said, 'Now, I have finished with the first part of my sermon and am ready to start the second part.' When I heard that, I felt that God was telling me to finish the first part of my life."

Preachers do what they can. God often acts because of that, and sometimes in spite of it. Sermons are like copper wiring. God is like electricity. God can move over inadequate conductors, and sometimes even jumps across gaps.

TURNING ON THE LIGHTS

Early one evening, when Robert Louis Stevenson was a small boy, he stood looking out the window onto a dark street.

Watching the lamplighter as he lighted the gas street lamps, he said, "I see something wonderful. I see a man coming up the street poking holes in the dark!"[6]

Preaching accomplishes many things, but its most basic task is to light lamps in dark mental corners. When church members repeat those old cliches that describe preaching as "getting your battery charged," they are speaking out of genuine experience. They have learned that preaching sometimes enables them to rise from the mud and reach for the stars because they suddenly see things a new way, from a new angle.

The most important coming of Christ was not in a Bethlehem stable. Nor will his Second Coming be the major event. The really important coming of Christ is his "continued coming" into our lives. Preaching is one of the times when that is most likely to happen. Preaching is where the Word, through spoken words, often becomes our word. When that happens, especially if it happens repeatedly, the lights of spiritual growth come on and stay on.

Chapter 8

ON THE
SERVING LINES

A young reporter, interviewing Mother Teresa after she had received the Nobel Peace Prize, commented, "I understand that people are dying by the thousands over there. Why do you just go around and help one here and one there?"

This woman, who gave her life to the dying people in the streets of Calcutta, picking them up and nursing them back to health, replied, "Young man, I do what I can, where I am, with what I have."

On another occasion, Leighton Ford asked Mother Teresa what she would say if she could speak to a gathering of evangelists from across the world.

She answered, "Be holy and love one another."[1]

In both conversations, Mother Teresa was articulating a basic biblical principle: People who connect with God also connect with other people in service. When a young man asked Jesus for the secret to spiritual maturity, Jesus told him to love God and his neighbor (Mark 12:30-31). On another occasion, Jesus told his disciples, "Whoever wishes to be great among you must be your servant, and whoever wishes to be first among you must be your slave; just as the Son of Man came not to be served but to serve, and to give his life a ransom for many" (Matt. 20:26b-28). Contemporary research supports that biblical evidence. Persons who frequently experience a sense of communion with God are "significantly more likely to value helping others."[2]

This strong correlation between serving others and spirituality is more powerful than many pastors perceive. *Laypeople usually rank service ahead of Bible study when they list the experiences that have facilitated their spiritual growth.* Service is apparently somewhat like tuning our TV to God's channel. Helping others does not *guarantee* spiritual growth (distracted by other preoccupations, we may not watch the program), but serving puts us in a frame of mind that makes it possible. American poet Archibald MacLeish said, "Man can live his truth, his deepest truth, but he cannot speak it. It is for this reason that love becomes the ultimate human answer to the ultimate human question."[3] In serving others, we can both experience that answer and move closer to the God whose nature is love (I John 4:16).

MASTERING LIFE

Service opens the doors of our minds to the mind of Christ in several ways. First, serving helps us to overcome our natural tendency toward selfishness—which is opposite to the nature of God. In *Have This Mind,* Bishop Gerald Kennedy describes a professor who was "fundamentally nuts"—he was crazy about himself![4] People easily drift into that kind of insanity if they fail to find anything other than themselves on which to center their lives. Serving is one of the ways we can take the first step outside the walls of ourselves.

A woman came to a renowned rabbi after years of counseling. Nothing had helped. She gave him an eight-page analysis of her problem. He told her to go back to her college campus and start taking action instead of just thinking. He instructed her to begin by making it a habit to serve other people during meals.

"Whatever it is that someone else might need," he said, "the butter, the sugar, the salt, a glass of water, whatever it is, it should become your habit to bring it to them." Looking back later, she saw this small change in behavior as her first step away from being a selfish, egotistical person.[5]

The more you give, the more you receive is more than a religious admonition; it is a spiritual law of the universe (see Mark 4:24). The British cynic Cyril Connolly was, to a large extent, both accurate and biblical when he said, "We are all serving a life sentence in the dungeon of self."[6] Serving others can help dungeon residents, imprisoned in their own littleness, to pick the lock on the cell of self and walk toward the sunshine.

Paradoxically, as we move away from our self-center, our self-esteem increases. One pastor said that he has discovered what to do when he gets tangled in a low-grade depression. He visits people. By extending his concern to people who are hurting, he comes up out of "the pits" every time. Many others have learned that truth: Few people can stay negative about themselves while actively caring about other people.

As we move beyond the small circle of our self-centeredness and gain self-esteem, we increasingly see the value of "mastership." More than 260 times, the New Testament describes followers of Christ as *disciples.* That label means "learner," but the learning involves much more than mastering a block of information. A disciple masters life by experiencing the mastership of Christ (John 13:13). And a prime ingredient of that mastership is service.

At his Gethsemane experience, the night before the cross, Jesus did not ask the disciples to pray, but to come and *be with him.* That is the essence of spirituality—being with Christ— and serving is one of the ways we can do that.

THREE-WAY SERVING

Service that furthers spiritual growth can take place in three different ways: (1) direct service to people; (2) service to people through the church; and (3) service that helps the church empower others to serve.

Direct Service to People. Examples would include various kinds of Good Samaritan gestures—from helping a stranded motorist to Cancer Fund contributions. One woman finds spiritual meaning in playing the piano twice a month during the dinner hour at a nursing home, and by visiting a blind girl. By tapping this human instinct for helping others, Habitat for Humanity provides low-cost housing for countless families who could otherwise never own a home. Much of every congregation's best service occurs completely outside its organizational supervision.

Service to People Through the Church. Among the many forms of this kind of service, financial stewardship is one of the most meaningful. Laypeople rank "giving money to help with God's work in the world" seventh, *immediately after Bible study,* as a facilitator of spiritual growth. Pastors, by contrast, rank financial stewardship eleventh on the list of twelve—revealing one of the reasons many pastors are less than enthusiastic about this aspect of their leadership role. They do not see the giving of dollars from the same spiritual perspective as do their parishioners. Clergy do not seem to grasp as clearly as laypeople the enormous truths in Jesus' teaching about money: "Give, and it will be given to you . . . for the measure you give will be the measure you get back (Luke 6:38*a, c*). Laypeople understand that one of the meaningful ways they can serve is through the financial support of people who can go where they cannot go—locally, nationally, and across the world—and serve on their behalf.

Teaching is the next most frequently mentioned source of spiritual growth in this category. The old adage that teachers learn more than those they teach seems true for many disciples. Teaching a Sunday school class or sponsoring a youth group is often a significant step on the road to God. For countless persons, the gift of teaching is indeed a gift, not just for upbuilding the church but also for upbuilding the spiritual life of the receiver (see I Cor. 12:28).

For some people, evangelism-focused service facilitates their own spiritual growth. Like Jesus when he helped the lame man, they want to help people spiritually as well as physically (see Mark 2:5, 11). In ways appropriate to their temperament and circumstances, these kinds of disciples attempt to "go therefore and make [other] disciples" (Matt. 28:19).

At a church whose attendance has soared to more than 5,000 in the past several years, the mission statement regards every member as a minister whose mission is to (a) lead people to faith in Christ; (b) grow in the love of Christ; (c) serve in the name of Christ; and (d) lift up praise to Christ. Why is evangelism the first item on that spiritual-maturity list? When we influence others to move toward Christ, we ourselves move closer to Christ, becoming more empowered to love, serve, give, and praise.

Action Possibilities

- A church lives out its activity as "the Body of Christ" through worship, preaching, evangelism, education, stewardship, Bible study, prayer, fellowship, and service. List those nine words on a sheet of paper or a chalkboard. Then, telling them not to sign their names, ask each member of the church governing body to arrange those nine words on a piece of paper, placing at the top of the list those aspects they think are most emphasized in their congregation. Collect the sheets and collate the answers by counting the number of times each word appears in each rank from the top to the bottom—numbering the top rank 1, the second rank 2, and so forth. If "service" was ranked low on this list, consider ways you might change that emphasis.
- The road traveled by the Good Samaritan in Jesus' parable now leads to the ends of the earth. The evening news connects TV viewers to pain in every part of the world. If we

are not trying in some way to alleviate some of that pain, can we call ourselves caring disciples of Jesus Christ?

Ask the appropriate committee to designate, each year, one to three "crisis needs" across the world as ministries to which they will encourage the people in the congregation to give. (These decisions cannot, of course, be made in advance; they must be made one at a time, by the appropriate church committee, as the year unfolds and world news makes us aware of crisis needs.) After the funds are secured from volunteers who wish to help with this particular need, dedicate the dollars in a morning worship service. Publicize what has been accomplished in the next week's worship bulletin and church newsletter.

Service That Helps the Church Empower Others to Serve. The service voltage of Christian disciples is maintained and enhanced by a power station called the institutional church. Servanthood directed toward maintaining and strengthening the vitality of this central power station can also be a source of personal spiritual growth for those who lead and maintain it.

Prominent among these roles, of course, is service as a pastor. For many disciples, spiritual growth comes through the role of preparing sermons, caring about church members, and equipping the laity for their daily lives.

Among service roles directed toward strengthening the church as an institutional server, leadership and administration are the next most frequently mentioned sources of spiritual growth.

"Leadership" is the gift of spiritual vision that helps Christians to set goals congruent with God's will and to communicate these goals in ways that cause others to work voluntarily and harmoniously toward their achievement (I Tim.; Heb. 13:17). Leadership roles in the church facilitate spiritual growth to the degree that they are seen as spiritual service—rather than as mere church offices. This is surely why church offices are mentioned only three times in the New Testament (Acts 1:20; Col. 1:25; and I Tim. 3:1)—while numerous texts refer to various roles of service for church leaders.

"Administration" is the gift of clearly understanding the goals of a particular section of church life and executing effectively designed plans for the accomplishment of these goals (I Cor. 12:28; Acts 6:1-7). As with the gift of leadership, the degree to which administrative service facilitates spiritual growth varies widely—depending upon the degree to which the role is seen as spiritual service, rather than as filling a slot in the organizational machine. Church administration roles that aim at realizing the mind of Christ in every set of circumstances can be a powerful source of spiritual growth.

Action Possibilities

• Does our church focus on involving people in actually doing ministry, rather than merely in holding church offices and serving on committees?

Only about 15 to 30 percent of church members feel comfortable in visionary and administrative roles. More than anything else, this is due to the predisposition of visionaries and administrators to enjoy using verbal and conceptual skills. Most of the other 70 to 85 percent of persons in each church are workers. They desire to serve in some way, but they feel more comfortable *doing things* than in serving on committees, where the focus is on using verbal and conceptual skills to *discuss things.*

This is one of the reasons many churches report that the maximum involvement of people in genuine service occurred: (a) during a building program; (b) during the years when the church first started and was meeting in a school; or (c) when there were annual bazaars, or some other organized effort that involved a great volume of work. During those periods, *every type of person* felt that he or she was capable of helping and could be involved in a meaningful way.

How can a church move back in that direction, thus giving more people opportunities to experience spiritual growth through service? One of the best ways is to shift our focus away from trying to get people to "serve on committees" and toward trying to get them involved in ministries. The following steps can help to accomplish that objective. The time line is designed for a calendar-year church-officer cycle. Congregations that elect officers at other times of the year should alter the time line accordingly.

1. In June, ask each committee to make a list of all the specific ministry tasks and functions in the church that logically belong under its supervision. (List *everything*, from singing in the choir to caring for the rose garden. Include even the smallest, least obvious tasks and roles.)

2. In August, collect these lists of ministry tasks and functions, and collate them on a couple of sheets of paper (the list will contain between 40 and 150 items).

3. During September, October, or November, plan a one-month "Spiritual Gifts Emphasis."

4. During the first two weeks of that emphasis, in all adult Sunday school classes and in as many other groups as possible, use one of the many spiritual-gift inventory processes available through various sources (see the Resource Section). Do not use any process of this type every year. Use it during the first year of this approach for involving members in ministry—and every five to seven years thereafter.

5. During the third week, the pastor preaches a sermon lifting up the idea that your church is in the business of doing Christ's work, and each of your church's "ministries" is a chance for each of us to answer Christ's call. Use one of the following scriptures as a text: Romans 12:1-8; I Corinthians 12:1-27 and 14:1-5; Ephesians 4:1-7, 11-16; or I Peter 4:8-11.

6. Although some congregations focus on stewardship of talents and money at the same time, emphasizing both of these at once tends to weaken the results in both areas. Generally speaking, it is wiser to focus on them separately—

with at least six weeks between the spiritual-gifts emphasis and the financial-stewardship program.

7. During morning worship on the last Sunday of the one-month "Spiritual Gifts Emphasis," distribute handout sheets and give worshipers the opportunity to indicate the areas of church life in which they feel God has gifted them and is calling them to serve this year. (This sheet contains the list of ministry tasks developed in June by the committees, as well as a place for signature, address, and phone number.) Do *not* let people take the sheets home and return them next week. Rather, set aside five minutes during the worship service for their completion.

8. In December or January—just prior to or just after the beginning of the new program year—the committee chairpeople meet and examine the sheets the people have completed. Working as a team, the chairpeople decide: (a) which persons will be asked to serve on their committees; and (b) which persons will be asked to work in the particular ministry roles and tasks for which their committees are responsible. Three to seven persons (depending on the size of the congregation) are invited to serve on each standing committee. The illusion that every church member wants to, or should be asked to, attend committee meetings must be discarded.

9. When the committees meet for the first time in January, they focus on developing a strategy to accomplish the ministries for which each committee is responsible that year—by involving many persons in: (a) serving on specific "teams"; (b) working on specific "short-term projects"; and (c) doing specific "tasks." They will not, however, expect all those individuals to attend committee meetings.

a. The "teams" consist of persons who feel gifted for and called to service in a particular aspect of church life. The teams serve all year (morning-worship greeters are one example of such a team; choir members are another example).

b. One example of a "short-term project" in some churches would be organizing, planning, and executing the annual Thanksgiving dinner, or some event of that type. When the project is completed, the job ends.

c. One example of a specific "task" in some churches would be ordering flowers for special days all year.

10. Each committee includes a much broader group of persons from the congregation as it accomplishes the ministries of the church. Thus, the committees see themselves more as supervisory and policy-making groups than as "the people who do all the work." The committee members certainly do some of the work, but their most important job is to involve other people in the congregation in specific activities.

Church leaders who think they can "do this ourselves" more easily than they can involve and train other people are practicing a deceptive logic that is destructive to congregational health and to the spiritual growth of members. In the short term, doing it yourself feels easier. But over a period of years, doing it yourself results in burnout, a smaller attendance at committee meetings, and a general feeling that "a few people do everything around here." Leaders do Christians a real service by involving them in the opportunity to develop their own skills and enjoy the feeling of success at accomplishing important church ministries. *Involve, delegate, supervise, appreciate*—these four words can form a picture frame around the new life that can come into both churches and people.

The how-to application of the above-described principle in a large, fast-growing congregation is helpfully illustrated in *Every Member in Ministry*, by John Ed Mathison. (See the Resource Section for ways obtain this and other books that describe methods based on the same principle.)

• Do we have a systematic way of helping our new members to consider what gifts God is calling them to use in the church's ministry?

Many churches expect their new members to become actively involved in service within the church, but have no real plan for helping that to happen. Therefore, only about 30 percent of new members end up in jobs or roles for which they are spiritually gifted and psychologically suited. As a result, many either drop out of church or function at a very low level of productivity—which may then lead to a feeling of overload and burnout in the long-term members who desperately need help.

The small congregation should train a volunteer who assumes responsibilities for new-member involvement. The large congregation, where hundreds of people may join each year, needs a part-time lay-staff person for this role. Whatever method you select, do not send out "Talent and Interest" inventories in the mail, or leave them in the home to be returned later, or distribute them at a new-member dinner and expect them to be returned later. These nonproductive methods are among the most important reasons so few members become involved in church ministries and roles. (See the Resource Section for tools that empower new-member assimilation.)

• Do we seem to strike a good balance between serving human physical need and spiritual needs, of which evangelism is a major example?

Review the past year's church calendar and church newsletters. Activities generally fall into three categories: (a) activities that serve our members through worship, teaching, and fellowship; (b) activities that help our members serve the spiritual needs of people in the community through various evangelistic reach-out efforts; and (c) activities that help our members serve the physical and emotional needs of people in the community through "hands-on" and financial helping efforts. Which of these three categories seems to be the most under-represented in our church calendar and newsletter last year? What can we do about that?

A researcher who studied several churches that were experiencing new health and vitality observed that each had become "a two-armed church with a strong heart." Their two arms are evangelism and social action. Their strong heart is shown in worship, preaching, nurture, and education.[7] That picture also accurately describes churches that effectively facilitate the spiritual growth of their members through service opportunities.

THE BOTTOM LINE

An Australian truck driver was steering his giant eighteen-wheeler along the crowded streets of downtown Melbourne. Creeping along in rush-hour traffic, he saw a girl limping down the sidewalk. For three blocks, he watched her uneven gait. Then, right in the middle of a block, he stopped his big rig, hopped down out of the cab, and ran over to her.

"Girl," he said, "I have the same kind of ailment you have."

When he named it, she said, "Yes, that is what I have."

"I found a wonderful doctor who can cure you," he told her. After scribbling down the doctor's name, he gave her the scrap of paper, climbed back into his truck, and drove away.

Having the mind of Christ results in living the actions of Christ. People who have Christ in their heads give Christ through their lives. Few Christians become a Mother Teresa, and not too many become pastors. But every Christian has opportunities every day to serve—and by that service, to grow spiritually closer to the mind of Christ.

Chapter 9

FOLLOWING
THE PAPER TRAIL

A railroad worker in India found a page from the Gospel of John. When he read some of the words, he said, "This is what I need." From a fellow worker, he learned about a church he could attend. That day, his life was pointed in a new direction.

A man in a motel opened a Gideon Bible. Near suicide and desperate for help, he began to read. Suddenly, he saw another way and resolved to move in that direction.

Few people report receiving such instantaneous and dramatic biblical guidance. But many people list the Bible as a source of spiritual growth. By reporting how others were empowered by a God connection, the Bible provides a paper trail for contemporary travelers. Speed-reading is a valuable skill, but speed-thinking is even better. The Bible is a portable classroom for taking a course of that kind.

Preparing to flee a hurricane warning, a family packed to leave. They knew they might not see their home standing again. With only the car's trunk to transport belongings, what would they take? The family picture album was among the items they chose. For Christians, the Bible is like that family album. This collection of faith stories makes up the big story of the way people connect with God and grow in that relationship.

COMPASS POWER

The Bible fulfills its role in several ways. Among the most important of these ways is the authority it lends to our spiritual journeys.

Fishermen in a small boat went to their favorite spot, about five miles from the coast. In the late afternoon, a dense fog moved in, catching them off guard. They started back too late. Land was now invisible. After several moments of panic, one of them remembered an old compass in the bottom of his tackle box.

The pointer told them to go a direction different from the one their instincts had chosen. Desperate, they decided to trust the authority in that tiny sliver of metal, and at long last, the shadowy outline of land emerged through the mist. The dock from which they had departed was only a few yards away.

Every endeavor, from fishing to dentistry to space science, needs an authority base of reliable information. Spiritual growth is no exception. People who find their way home to the mind of Christ must head in the right direction. Thus, Paul's advice to one of his churches is still important: "Let the word of Christ dwell in you richly" (Col. 3:16). The biblical record is the only dependable source of the words that Christ spoke. This paper trail is not the shoreline—Christ, not a book, is the goal of faith—but the words on these pages provide authoritative advice for moving in his direction.

ROAD-MAP POWER

As well as telling us in what direction to go, the Bible provides travel tips. After we connect with Christ, we want to grow in his view of God, of people, and of truth and error. Scripture is a road map for this continuing journey. Thus the apostle Paul says, "All scripture is inspired by God and is useful for teaching, for reproof, for correction, and for training in righteousness" (II Tim 3:16). The other spiritual-growth basics are important—worship, music, prayer, fellowship, preaching, and service—but you cannot hold them in your hand. No wonder almost everyone owns a Bible, and many display it in a place of honor—even though they may never read it. No other spiritual-growth source is as visible and tangible.

In giving the Bible its due tribute, we must not, however, jump to the wrong conclusion. Biblical information is not the prime objective of the Christian faith. Disciples are not defined by what they know, but by whether they think, talk, and act like Christ. People with the most Bible knowledge are not necessarily the best Christians—any more than the people who own road maps always decide on the right destination. The New Testament therefore seldom uses the word *teach* to mean transmitting a block of religious information. To *teach* means to make disciples. Yet, the New Testament provides a reliable paper trail of footprints. By their description of Christ's actions and words, they can lead us to the mind of Christ.

FROM INFORMATION TO TRANSFORMATION

Negus Menelik, who ruled Ethiopia from 1889 to 1913, believed that the Bible had magical power. Each day, he ate two pages! This worked well until he came to some color illustrations. The chemicals used in the coloring were poisonous, and he died.[1]

If the Bible is not magic, exactly how does it help people grow spiritually? How does the information on these pages become transformational in the reader's life? It does this in at least three ways.

1. **The written word renders Christ present.** Jesus said good-bye to the disciples at the last supper. In the words of Scripture, he says hello and becomes present again. As we study and discuss these words, Christ appears and walks with

us, as he did with the disciples on the road to Emmaus, following his resurrection.

During a highway construction project in England, the excavations threw up to the surface soil that had not been exposed for centuries. Some of the flowers that came up that spring could have come only from seeds brought there by the Romans, since those flowers had never been seen in England, but are common in Rome. Things like that happen every day through the written word. People read, and faith in Christ comes alive as Christ becomes present with them.

2. **The written word lets God speak to our changing experiences and circumstances.** Its words do not change, so why should we read the Bible more than once? Because our experiences and circumstances change. At a different time in our life, the old information becomes totally new to us. That is why the Bible instructs us to meditate on God's Word. When we read it through the lens of new circumstances, we often find in it a divine mirror (James 1:23-25), a lamp to our feet (Ps. 119:105), and a taste sweeter than honey (Ps. 19:10).

Another reason for rereading the Bible: We are not always ready to listen the first time it speaks to us. One woman summed up her attitude toward Jesus Christ during her teenage and young-adult years by an experience she had at age six. She was visiting some relatives who lived on a farm. While exploring, she became fascinated by a red-ant bed. Having never seen anything like this, she watched the ants closely while they crawled up her shoes and swarmed over her socks. Her fascination ended when they reached her bare legs.

"The whole thing was such a shock that all I could do was stand there and scream. My older brother heard me from a distance and yelled, 'Don't just stand there—stomp your feet!' and I yelled back, 'You can't tell *me* what to do!'"

Rereading the Bible lets God speak to us at a time when we are ready to listen—which may not be the first time.

3. **The written word protects us from distortions of spiritual truth.** The Christian faith is a set of ideas about life at its best

through a relationship with God. Together, these pearls make the necklace of personal faith bright and beautiful. What if a jeweler with poor eyesight drills holes in white marbles and substitutes them for some of the pearls? The necklace becomes something less than *Christian* faith. That, in fact, repeatedly happens. Pagan ideas are always wandering around in church and society, disguised as biblical Christianity. Continuous Bible study helps disciples distinguish marbles from pearls.

FROM INCLINATIONS TO CONSUMMATIONS

When the written word passes into the mind and results in new behaviors, spiritual growth takes place. This happens through hearing (Rom. 10:17), reading (Rev. 1:3), studying (Acts 17:11), memorizing (Ps. 119:9, 11), and meditating (Ps. 1:2-3). The rubber of those spiritual-growth facilitators hits the road in one or more of three primary ways.

1. Books That Illustrate Biblical Truth. A surprising percentage of Christians report that reading books other than the Bible—books that illustrate the Bible's spiritual truth—is a catalyst that helps them grow spiritually. Comments such as the following exemplify their experiences:

• "Reading inspirational religious books."
• "Books encouraging spiritual growth."
• "Reading other spiritual books."
• "Writings of the experts (saints); specialty areas."
• "Reading challenging articles and books."

The strong role of literature written about the Bible is consistent with other information from the study that forms the basis for this book. For a majority of people, preaching is a stronger spiritual-growth facilitator than Bible study. Interpretation and illustration obviously help biblical truth to come alive. For many people, books about the Bible apparently fulfill a role similar to that of oral sermons.

2. **Solitary Bible Study.** In a recent cartoon, a teenager is talking to a friend on the phone: "I think I've made a great step toward unraveling the mysteries of the Old Testament. I'm starting to read it." Many people concur with that conclusion. Once they establish the discipline of daily Bible study, they experience spiritual growth. The following comments that describe its catalytic influence exemplify countless other statements from survey respondents:

• "Personal Bible study."
• "Reading through the Bible systematically."
• "Personal Bible reading."

Spiritual growth is not something we can create instantly, like turning on a light switch. But Bible reading can create conditions in which the experience is more likely to happen. Someone once asked a saintly man which he thought was more important—Bible study or private prayer. The man replied with another question: "Which do you consider the more important to a bird—the right wing or the left?"[2] Like prayer, the story line of the Bible is so powerful that it can pull us into the story and God into us.

3. **Group Bible Study.** Group Bible study has great potential for facilitating spiritual growth (more than one-fourth of Americans are involved in a Bible study group of some type). Many people identify the origins of their spiritual growth with words similar to those of one pastor: "Small groups concentrating on Bible study and living our faith daily have been high points."

Action Possibility Questions

• Do our church's adult Sunday school and other Bible study groups maintain a balanced emphasis in their discussions?

The dynamics of group Bible study are like a pyramid sliced by two horizontal lines. The bottom section symbolizes the basic biblical material (historical setting, who wrote to whom, why, when, where, etc.). The middle section of the pyramid symbolizes the way that biblical material applies to people in our current society. The top slice of the pyramid symbolizes the way that biblical material applies to the personal life of each study-group member.

Effective study groups deal with all three layers of the Bible's message: its historical aspects, its present-day applications to society, and its personal applications to individuals. Groups become ineffectual when they lose their balance and emphasize one section of the pyramid to the exclusion of the other two. Some, for example, bog down in biblical exegesis. Under the leadership of an avid Bible-student teacher, they spend all their time on textual minutia, such as, "*When* did Paul write the letter to the Corinthians?" The class session seems like one hour of commentary. It never gets out of the Bible onto the sidewalk of contemporary life. Too much of this produces a result like the answer from the back of the room following a tedious lesson about Jonah and the whale. When the teacher asked what we can learn from the story, someone said, "Travel by air!"

Other groups bog down in the middle section of the pyramid. They seem like a sociology class because they never get off the sidewalk. A good example of this pattern is the adult class in a small country church, where the "welfare problem" is discussed every Sunday morning. Because one of the class members has a fixation on this subject, he always brings it up and keeps the class focused on it. Visitors are repelled by this negative, boring atmosphere. This class is cemented in one particular square of the sidewalk. The teacher has forgotten that the objective of Bible study is not philosophical idea exchange. Group Bible study that is spiritually effective is not just idea-changing; it is life-changing.

Another kind of group gets stuck on the pyramid's top section—personal application. This pattern was common in the "group therapy" type studies of the late 1960s. Many groups became emotional strip-tease shows, where people shared the intimate details of their lives and felt very close to one another in the process. Warmth and acceptance ran high, but the groups eventually became introverted cliques incapable of accepting outsiders. They finally ran out of things to share, as group members kept repeating the same feelings about each new text they studied.

Contemporary disciples have the advantage of countless different Bible translations, but the best version is the one by which we allow our lives to be remolded *this week*. Effective group leaders try to keep people focused on present-life application (in contrast to endless repetition of "how it has always worked with me"). This concentrates the group's attention on the Word of God now, instead of the Word of God *for yesterday*.

• Do our church's adult Sunday school and other Bible study groups use some sort of evaluation mechanism that allows them to pinpoint their strengths and weaknesses in a nonthreatening way?

The evaluation exercise shown on page 116 has more value for discussion classes than for those using the lecture method, but it can provide insights for any group. Use the evaluation sheets every six months. Ask class members to fill them out without discussing the questions among themselves. After the sheets are completed, collect them and total up the three kinds of answers given for each question. List the composite figures on a flip chart or chalkboard. This allows class members to express their opinions about class dynamics in a constructive way. It helps the teacher and class steering committee to sense problems and take action to correct them before they begin to hurt the class. The tabulated results also give the individual class members clues into ways their own participation can improve the quality of the class experience for all members.

• Does our church use one or more of the many models and curriculum available for group Bible study?

EVALUATING OUR CLASS CLIMATE

Please indicate your opinion by writing yes, no, or sometimes.
(No names, please; just be honest.)

_____	1. The leader keeps the discussion moving in such a way that it does not bog down in useless speculation.
_____	2. Everyone enters the discussion.
_____	3. Differing points of view are accepted.
_____	4. The discussion emphasizes experiences, feelings, and opinions, rather than theories.
_____	5. The leader tends to dominate the discussion.
_____	6. One individual in the group (other than the leader) tends to dominate the discussion each time.
_____	7. All members prepare for the discussion before they arrive.
_____	8. The members of the group are honest with one another.
_____	9. I feel completely relaxed and at ease in the discussion.
_____	10. We tend to bog down in "what other people do wrong."
_____	11. There is an honest effort on the part of the members to see how the topic applies to them, rather than how it applies to others in the church (or outside the church).
_____	12. I find the discussions personally helpful.
_____	13. The group members seem to be genuinely concerned about one another.
_____	14. The group bogs down in speculation about what various experts, scholars, and ministers say.
_____	15. I could honestly recommend this kind of group to one of my close friends.

You can begin by organizing at least two home groups. (Unless you have two groups, a small church's Bible study may turn into another meeting of the same primary social group.) Handpick people to take part. Make sure they realize that you expect them to duplicate the process by starting another group next year.

Numerous excellent materials are available—both for developing the group models and for study content. (See the Resources Section for a list.)

THE EARTH IS MOVING

When Albert Einstein visited the Long Beach campus of the University of California in March of 1933, his host from the geology department gave him a tour of the campus. The two fell into animated conversation, intently discussing the motions of earthquakes. They became puzzled when they noticed all the people running out of the campus buildings. While deep in thought regarding seismology, they had not noticed the earthquake that was occurring under their feet.[3]

Something similar is happening in congregations. *Time* magazine says that young adults are rediscovering the Bible.[4] Highly conscious that "you are what you eat," this generation knows that better eating habits can reduce the risk of death from heart attacks and cancer by 50 percent. Many of them also believe that they can reduce the risk of living distant from God by consuming more appropriate spiritual food.

The bad news: Many mainline church leaders seem oblivious to this keen interest and fail to provide appropriate Bible-study opportunities. This makes congregations grow gradually older and smaller, in emptier buildings.

The good news: Congregations whose leaders feel this seismographic change and take action find their buildings increasingly filled—and their people increasingly filled by the spiritual growth that comes from following the biblical paper trail.

Chapter 10

THE ENCOURAGING WORD

A t a critical point in her life, a young woman was not sure what direction her career should take. Then a coffee conversation with a respected mentor gave her the self-confidence to move past her uncertainty. Years later, she still remembers those words: "You have enough intelligence and ability to succeed at whatever you want to do. Decide which of these options you feel makes the most sense, and go for it." For her, those words were "apples of gold in a setting of silver" (Prov. 25:11).

Many travelers on the road of spiritual growth report experiences of that sort as important aspects of their trip. On the opinion-poll list of possible growth facilitators which served as a basis for this book, *encouragement* ranked after worship, music, prayer, fellowship, service, sermons, and Bible study.

However, spiritual encouragement differs from other kinds of encouragement in one major way: People who provide words of spiritual encouragement often find themselves growing spiritually as part of the process.

Many people cited one or both of these two kinds of encouragement as the major element in their spiritual-growth experiences: (1) For some, encouraging other people through roles such as friend, pastor, counselor, or church leader brought a boomerang benefit. The words they gave to others doubled back to help them in their own spiritual journey. (2) For other people, the encouragement they received from others was the key factor in their spiritual growth. Parents, relatives, neighbors, pastors, Sunday school teachers, and friends (most of whom are ordinary people) played prominent roles in their experiences. Especially at life-crisis points, these important others became extraordinarily influential in strengthening a spiritual connection with God.

In spiritual genetics, we all receive the gift that was given to Paul by his associate. Barnabus, whose name means "son of encouragement," is somewhere in our spiritual genealogies. All of us are sons and daughters of encouragement, in that much of what we can become depends upon what others have said to us.

The stacks of opinion-poll responses indicate, however, that the first of the two experiences described above is most powerful. The most significant spiritual growth comes through the encouraging words we say to others, rather than what others say to us. When Paul advised, "Encourage one another and build up each other," he was also suggesting a potent means of strengthening the spiritual growth of the encourager (I Thes. 5:11). Contemporary disciples often experience that truth. In countless ways, they report that their words to others have added to their own spiritual strength, as we can see from some of their comments:

- "Hospital calling and dealing with terminal illness."
- "Pastoral love and counseling—helping others understand their lives and their relationships with God."
- "Visiting shut-ins who live alone; talking, but mostly listening; calling on the telephone; sending cards; taking small favors to them; taping the minister's sermons and delivering them to the shut-ins."

A restaurant customer noted the unusual name on the badge the waitress was wearing on her uniform: "Angel." Few people are named Angel, but everyone can be one. Through encouraging words, we can communicate to other people in ways that help them strengthen their connection with God.

When that happens, the *angel* (a word that means "messenger") also gets the message.

"ENCOURAGE" IS AN ACTIVE VERB

Word transmissions that help both sender and receiver to grow spiritually can take many forms, among which these five are especially powerful:

1. **Positive Presence.** We can improve the quality of our "presence" by conscious effort, in order to serve the following mental foods in every conversation with every person: Attention, Affirm, Ask, and Appreciate.

Attention—as contrasted with a *preoccupation with self* that asks others to give attention to us. Is the typical question of "How are you?" with which we open a conversation actually genuine? Is it followed by additional caring questions after the other person responds? Or does our conversation immediately change to "How I am" and elaborate on what has happened to me recently?

Affirm—as contrasted with *criticism* of individuals, organizations, and current events. Is what we typically say about other people negative or positive? Do we usually say something good about others? Or do we tend to say things we would not be likely to say if they were standing within earshot? When other people criticize someone in our presence, do we usually pile on another criticism? Or do we respond with something like, "But he/she does have some good qualities; for example . . ."? All people have both faults and virtues. The side of their personality coin which we choose to talk about defines our personality as much as it does theirs.

Ask—as contrasted with *tell.* Positive-presence people ask numerous questions about what other people think, listen carefully to the answers, and then ask more questions. Negative-presence people, even if they ask a question, often use it like a dump-truck lever—following it by several tons of their own opinions. Positive-presence people use their ears more than their mouths, even when they do not agree with everything the other person is expressing.

Appreciate—as contrasted with a strictly *"task focus"* on the project or activity under discussion. Some personalities are inclined to be people-oriented; others are more task-oriented. Yet, even a task-oriented person can develop the habit of expressing appreciation. People judge us as positive or negative personalities by the way we act toward them personally. Appreciation, or the lack of it, sends a strong signal.

2. **Tact.** Research indicates that a large percentage of relational failures between pastor and people comes from a simple lack of tact. The results we get from "always telling the truth" and from "telling the truth all the time, to everyone, all day, every day" are as different as salting a steak and dumping the whole salt shaker on it. One pastor says that most people need greater "S & N" skills—smile and nod. This involves restraining yourself from providing all the information you can think of on the subject under discussion.

During Texas floods, a radio news commentator said, "Be careful about driving through water. It takes only two feet of flowing water to carry away the average car." Nor does it take a large volume of words to carry the average person away from churches. In most conversations, there is a vast difference between what *could* be said and what *should* be said. The wise leader has enough adhesive on his or her tongue to live out the difference between "could" and "should."

3. **Time.** Sending the signal that we are too busy to talk does much relational damage. Facial and body language that shows, "I don't have time to talk with you" is like holding up a sign that says, "You are not important!" Love is a four-letter word, spelled T-I-M-E.

One pastor tells about a period of several weeks in which he was overcommitted. His youngest daughter, having picked up on his habits, said one evening at dinner, "Daddy-I-wanna-tell-you-somethin'-and-I'll-tell-you-really-fast." Sensing her frustration, he answered that she could tell him and could say it slowly. "Then listen slowly," she suggested.[1]

People can tell whether we have time for them as easily as they can see a toad perched on our shoulder, ready to hop. Listening is a communication skill that we get the chance to use only after people sense that we care enough to take the time. People who transmit that impression practice a relaxed attentiveness when others speak. They have learned that attentive body and facial language require no additional time, and send a strong, positive signal of acceptance and affirmation.

4. **Listening.** Not everyone can be a teacher or a choir director or a pastor or a theologian. Not everyone can speak prophetically or lead some courageous crusade for the betterment of humanity. But everyone can perform the ministry of "standing by"—of being creatively, compassionately present with a listening ear. And when it comes to helping people handle the tough obstacles that life sets in their way, few powers exceed that of the listening ear, attached to a caring mind.

Effective listeners operate from two basic principles, of which less capable listeners seem unaware: (a) The prime objective of effective listening is not to hear enough information to offer a solution. Rather, effective listening allows the other person to hear his or her own information clearly enough to find insights and self-direction; (b) Listening to people in a nonjudgmental way—without offering evaluations or criticisms of their thinking, words, or behavior—does not equal giving approval of their inaccuracies, mistakes, or wrongdoings. Rather, effective listening accepts what people are saying, without a response that gives either approval or disapproval. Unless the listener understands and is emotionally comfortable with those two principles, training a person in effective listening is like teaching music to the tone deaf.

Effective listeners, either by instinct or by intention, avoid the five traits of poor listeners: (a) helping people finish sentences when they pause too long; (b) doing all the talking; (c) stepping on sentences by starting to talk before people have finished expressing their thoughts; (d) not maintaining eye contact while others are talking; and (e) giving more feedback than necessary by going too far beyond simple "uh huh's."[2] When a listener's conversational habit patterns include any of those five traits, people will enjoy talking to him or her about as much as hearing chalk screech on a blackboard.

The *desire* to listen and to understand is the single most important factor in accomplishing effective listening. When that desire is present, people can learn the fundamentals in a few minutes. Perfecting the skill of listening, like learning any other new behavior, takes practice, but the basics are simple. A communication expert puts them this way:

Paraphrasing. This involves stating back to the person the meaning of what she or he has just said. Good paraphrasing begins with such phrases as the following:

- "What you are saying is that . . ."
- "You are saying . . ."
- "Are you saying . . . ?"
- "You feel that . . ."

Paraphrasing tells the listener whether his or her understanding is still on track or has accidently become derailed onto another subject. Paraphrasing also tells the other person that the listener cares enough to pay close attention.

Perception Checking. With this tool, we give back to the other person the feeling that he or she seems to be expressing. Here, the feedback often involves sentences beginning with the personal pronoun "I":

- "I sense that . . ."
- "I hear you saying that you feel . . ."
- "I see that you are coming from a perspective of . . ."

Perception checking ensures that the listener understands the feelings and viewpoint behind the information the other person is conveying.

Creative Questioning. Good listeners use this tool to flush out missing information and give the other person permission to share in greater depth and detail. The creative question must not, however, seem like a judgment; if so, it will induce silent withdrawal instead of additional information. Nor can a genuinely creative question be answered with a simple yes or no. Creative questions express positive interest in receiving more information and also provide a receptive sliding board down which the person can send it.[3]

Avoiding the Sand Traps. Unskilled listeners often find themselves unexpectedly off the fairway. We can avoid many of these sand traps through increased awareness of the way we fall into them:

• Avoid giving advice such as, "If I were you, I would . . ." Instead, give the person time to arrive at the decision you think should be made, by using the active listening skills described above.

• Avoid trying to look as if you know everything. "I don't know" is an adequate answer to some of the direct questions from the person to whom you are listening.

• Avoid trying to be a psychiatrist with people who appear to be out of touch with reality, deeply depressed, or suicidal. If their problem seems to be an acute mental disorder of those types, encourage them to see a counselor or a physician.

• Avoid rushing in with prayer and Scripture readings, unless these seem quite appropriate on this occasion and with this individual.

• Avoid platitudes such as, "God helps those who help themselves." Platitudes communicate your lack of understanding that this person's problem is unique.

• Avoid using the other person's sharing of a problem as a chance to share a big problem of your own, thus changing the focus from his or her need to your need.

• Avoid arguing about facts and ideas. Few people are moved in positive directions by argumentation.

5. **Affirming Suggestions.** A pastor in West Texas saw twenty-eight young people enter the Christian ministry during his more than twenty years of service in that congregation. How was this possible? An excellent judge of abilities, he had mastered the "affirming suggestion." He did not hesitate to say, "I think you ought to consider becoming a minister. Have you given that possibility any thought?"

One of America's great teachers of preaching said that his life had been changed by suggestions from two important people. One was a high school teacher. The other was a pastor who encouraged him to attend college. Countless laypeople report similar experiences. They grew spiritually because someone encouraged them to serve on a committee, become a youth sponsor, teach a Sunday school class, or assume a church-officer role. "Let us consider how to provoke one another to love and good deeds" is more than a platitude (Heb. 10:24); it is often the key lubricant for people who move the world, move churches, and are themselves moved closer to God in the process.

ORGANIZED ENCOURAGEMENT

One of the major purposes of the "classes" in the renewal movement John Wesley began in England and America in the 1700s was "spiritual encouragement." This became a reality for millions of people because of Wesley's careful attention to developing organizational systems that were psychologically sound and fit the culture in which he served. Millions of Roman Catholics across the centuries have received spiritual encouragement in the confessional, a highly formalized procedure for facilitating caring, counseling, and spiritual direction. These illustrations spotlight an important principle: Much individual encouragement becomes possible only through congregational systems of organized encouragement.

Action Possibilities:

- At the close of each calendar year, organize a group of ten to twenty persons who are willing to regularly visit the housebound or people who have long-term illnesses. To recruit members, announce the shepherding program during worship services and publicize it in the church newsletter. On a specified date, make enrollment cards available during the morning worship services. Individuals who enroll become "shut-in shepherds" for one year. During that year, each shepherd regularly visits (in addition to telephoning and making contact on holidays, birthdays, and anniversaries) the person he/she has been assigned. Shepherds report to the church any illnesses or other significant information regarding the person for whom they have responsibility.
- Organize a Care Team of ten to twenty persons who meet monthly with the pastor(s) and accept assignments for visiting people who are ill, hospitalized, grieving, or suffering other stress. Avoid setting this up on a geographic basis: Those systems rarely work. If you divide the church into "flocks," allow Care Team members to select people for their flocks by taking turns picking up cards (with the names of all church families) from a table. Give the Care Team members time to report to one another about their work at each monthly meeting. Set up a system by which the church secretary automatically calls them when one of their group members is hospitalized or suffers bereavement. (See the Resource Section for two books to use in training Care Team members.)
- Many congregations are establishing a church "hot line" or "care line." This operates through an additional telephone line and an automatic answering machine. Each morning, one of the staff or the senior minister records two minutes of congregational information. This includes items such as

persons in the hospital, date and time of funerals, meetings, and events, a daily Scripture reading, and a prayer. Members of the congregation and others from the community soon begin calling every day for this information update. Such a care line accomplishes several important things: The congregation daily has the latest news about the church family, and the church secretary is saved hours of time by not having so many questions to answer.

The care line becomes one of the most current news sources in town and can sometimes be used to share needed information about community life. In times of emergency or bad weather, a fifteen-second tape can provide information about storm conditions or meeting cancellations.

- One church prints a graphic on cards, made up in many different colors. The cards are placed in the pew racks and on the tables during Wednesday-night dinners. People can write notes on them to persons who are ill or hospitalized and put them in the offering plate or drop them by the office. The church mails all the cards intended for a particular person in one envelope. The recipient thus gets a rainbow of colored cards with messages from many people.
- Some pastors use a calendar file to send birthday cards to members.
- Some pastors send a card or make a phone call to bereaved members on the day of the first anniversary of their loss.
- Some pastors, especially in large churches, set up a system for sending out a series of personal letters to new members, during the first six months or year after they join.
- In a Kansas church, the pastor telephones each child on the first day of school, just to talk about the experience.
- Some pastors write notes to several people each week on invitation-sized cards. Sometimes the subject is "I've missed you! Hope you are O.K., and we'll see you Sunday." At other times, the envelope might include a newspaper clipping about the person, with a note: "Congratulations! I read something good about you."

People will go a long way for encouragement. The influx of pilgrims to Knock, Ireland, where the Virgin is said to have appeared a century ago, swelled to the point that a new international airport was built. In a recent year, more than half a million people visited Emmitsburg, Maryland, one of the oldest of the forty-three shrines to Mary in the United States.[4] Disciples should not need to travel that far for encouragement. When church leaders appropriately organize to deliver it, disciples can find it without leaving town.

ENCOURAGEMENT IS IMMORTAL

Some years ago, a man decided to commit suicide by jumping off the Golden Gate Bridge in San Francisco. On the way there, his truck broke down. Changing his mind, he gave up the project, feeling that perhaps God did not want him to take his life. Soon, he visited a church about which he had heard good things. He was so warmly welcomed there that he returned the next week and committed his life to Christ.[5]

In a wind tunnel, engineers have calibrated what happens in the "V" formation used by Canadian geese. Each bird creates an upward lift for the one behind. This helps all the birds to conserve strength and gives them a 71 percent greater flying range than if each bird flew alone. Then, too, if one of the flyers begins to lag behind and drag the system, the others "honk" it back into place.

People who rise to the best that God has put within them seldom travel alone. If they go the distance of maximum spiritual growth toward the mind of Christ, somewhere along the way, someone gives them encouragement. And because they receive that word, they can pass it on to others.

Even the best bound books in history, printed on the best parchment, eventually disintegrate toward a dusty end. But encouraging words are eternal. This gift never stops giving. This chapter never ends. This book is never finished.

RESOURCES

The resources recommended in *Connecting with God* can be obtained from local bookstores, from denominational publishing houses, or through the addresses and phone numbers noted in this section.

You also may want to call or write the appropriate departments in the national or regional offices of your denomination for a listing of the resources they may produce in one or more of these ministry areas.

Chapter 1. GROPING FOR THE GOOD LIFE

The Upper Room publishes many excellent resources. Write P.O. Box 189, Nashville TN 37202-0189; phone 615/340-7227.

Chapter 3. WORSHIP IS JOB ONE

An excellent worship workshop is available each year at Community Church of Joy, Glendale, Arizona, an Evangelical Lutheran Church in America congregation. Write 16635 N. 51st Avenue, Glendale AZ 85306; phone 602/938-1460. Or you may wish to purchase the book based on this church's worship experience: *A Community of Joy: How to Create Contem-*

porary Worship by Timothy Wright (Nashville: Abingdon Press, 1994).

Middle-judicatory structures often sponsor a workshop titled "Effective Worship: Designing Services That Attract and Spiritually Enrich Contemporary Adults," led by Herb Miller. Contact the Net Results Resource Center, 5001 Avenue N, Lubbock TX 79412-2993; phone 806/762-8094. That workshop is also held at various locations throughout the United States each year—open to attenders from all denominations. Ask for NetWorkshops dates and locations.

Chapter 4. JOYFUL NOISES

Helpful resources for the development of choirs for youth and children are available in the audiotape *Developing Children, Youth, and Adult Choirs* by Bill Owens, available from Alpha Recording, Inc. (ask for the 1991 NEA Evangelism Conference Workshop tape #16), Attention: Jim Cottrell, 129 Howell Drive, P.O. Box 740, Elizabethtown KY 42701; phone 502/765-7899.

The book *Church Music Handbook for Pastors and Musicians* by N. Lee Orr (Nashville: Abingdon Press, 1991) contains practical resources for music leaders, pastors, and the staff-parish committees that hire, supervise, and evaluate church musicians. The appendix includes sample job descriptions, a recommended salary guide, sample contracts, and a worship planning sheet. Order from Cokesbury: 800/672-1789 or 615/749-6113.

Christian Copyright Licensing, Inc., provides permission, on a sliding fee scale, for churches to print songs, anthems, or choruses, either in their bulletin or on overhead transparencies. Write 6130 NE 78th Court, Suite C11, Portland OR 97218; phone 800/234-2446 or 503/257-2230.

Another excellent resource, *The Church Guide to Copyright Law,* is by Richard R. Hammar (Matthews, N. Car.: Christian Ministry Resources, 1990). Write Christian Ministry

Resources, P.O. Box 2301, Matthews NC 28106; phone 704/841-8066 or 800/222-1840.

Chapter 5. KEEPING IN TOUCH

Obtain the billfold-sized folder titled *The Secret to Abundant Living: Learning How to Ask.* Order from the Net Results Resource Center, 5001 Avenue N, Lubbock TX 79412-2993; phone 806/762-8094.

Obtain the inexpensive *How to Pray for Someone Else* packet by William Dudley Griffith from Fairway Press, 628 S. Main Street, Lima OH 45804; phone 800/537-1030 or 419/229-2665.

A variety of congregational prayer programs can be found in the action pac titled *Teach Us How to Pray,* edited by Herb Miller. Obtain from Net Results Resource Center, 5001 Avenue N, Lubbock TX 79412-2993; phone 806/762-8094.

Chapter 6. THE PEOPLE CONNECTION

The "how-to" action pac titled *Fellowship Evangelism,* edited by Herb Miller, has a proven formula for establishing a young-adult fellowship group with persons from both outside and inside the congregation. That action pac also describes effective procedures for seniors groups. Obtain from Net Results Resource Center, 5001 Avenue N, Lubbock TX 79412-2993; phone 806/762-8094.

The "how-to" action pac titled *Sunday School Development,* edited by Herb Miller, provides a formula for starting new adult classes in midsize and large churches. It also contains a formula for establishing new classes when the church building has insufficient space. Obtain from the Net Results Resource Center, 5001 Avenue N, Lubbock TX 79412-2993; phone 806/762-8094.

Obtain information on "The Walk to Emmaus" from The Upper Room, P.O. Box 189, Nashville TN 37202-0189; phone 615/340-7227.

Obtain information on "The Great Banquet" from Zionsville Presbyterian Church, 4775 W. 116th St., Zionsville IN 46077; phone 317/873-6503.

Obtain information on Roman Catholic Cursillo opportunities in your area from the National Center for the Cursillo Movement, P.O. Box 210226, Dallas TX 75211; phone 214/339-6321.

Obtain information on Episcopal Cursillo opportunities in your area from P.O. Box 213, Cedar Falls IA 50613-0213; phone 319/266-5323.

Obtain information on Lutheran Cursillo opportunities in your area from 421 W. Elk St., Geneseo IL 61254; phone 309/944-6904.

Obtain information on a two-day spiritual-growth event for pastors and church staff members from Herb Miller, Net Results Resource Center, 5001 Avenue N, Lubbock TX 79412-2993; phone 806/762-8094.

Obtain information on a one-day spiritual-growth event for laity, "Connecting With God: A Personal Renewal Experience That Equips Laity and Clergy to Strengthen Their Congregation's Ability to Help People Grow Spiritually" from Herb Miller, Net Results Resource Center, 5001 Avenue N, Lubbock TX 79412-2993; phone 806/762-8094.

Obtain information on the "Discovery Sunday" spiritual-growth program for congregations by Herb Miller, from Net Results Resource Center, 5001 Avenue N, Lubbock TX 79412-2993; phone 806/762-8094.

Chapter 7. TURNING ON THE LIGHTS

The audiotape *Oral Manuscript Preparation* by Clyde Fant describes an approach to sermon preparation and delivery that has proved instantly helpful to countless pastors of all ages and stages of preaching skill. Obtain from the Net Results Resource Center, 5001 Avenue N, Lubbock TX 79412-2993; phone 806/762-8094.

The audiocassette *Communicating the Message from the Sponsor to Television Society* by Haddon Robinson, one of America's premier teachers of preaching, describes in practical terms how to meet the challenge of communicating Christ to secular people who grew up absorbing much of their information from pictures rather than from print. Order from Convention Cassettes Unlimited, 41-550 Eclectic St., Suite C-140, Palm Desert CA 92260; phone 800/776-5454 or 619/773-4498.

Weekly drama scripts for worship services are available from Willow Creek Resources, Zondervan Publishing House, 5300 Patterson SE, Grand Rapids MI 49530; phone 800/876-7335 or 616/698-3230.

Chapter 8. ON THE SERVING LINES

Every Member in Ministry by John Ed Mathison is available from Discipleship Resources, P.O. Box 856, Nashville TN 37202; phone 615/340-7284. Mathison's concepts are available also in audiotape form titled "Effective Methods for Assimilating New Members," available from Alpha Recording, Inc. (ask for the 1991 NEA Evangelism Conference Workshop tape #13), Attention: Jim Cottrell, 129 Howell Drive, P.O. Box 740, Elizabethtown, KY 42701; phone 502/765-7899.

Careful scrutiny of books such as those on the following list can help leaders see the major differences between focusing on developing committees and focusing on involving persons in ministries: *Volunteer Ministries—New Strategies for Today's Church* by Margie Morris (available from Newton-Cline Press, 421 N. Sam Rayburn Freeway, Sherman TX 75090—phone 903/892-1818); *Recruiting, Training, and Developing Volunteer Adult Workers* by John Hendee (Standard Publishing, 8121 Hamilton Ave., Cincinnati OH 45231—phone 800/543-1353 or 513/931-4050); *Empowering Lay Volunteers* by Douglas W.

Johnson (Abingdon Press, P.O. Box 801, 201 8th Ave. S., Nashville TN 37202—phone 800-672-1789); and *How to Mobilize Church Volunteers* by Marlene Wilson (Augsburg Publishers, 426 S. Fifth St., Box 1209, Minneapolis MN 55440-1209— phone 800/328-4648 or 612/330-3300).

An excellent resource for helping to involve middle schoolers and youth in service is *Beyond Leaf Raking: Learning to Serve/Serving to Learn* by Peter Benson and Eugene Roehlkepartain (Nashville: Abingdon Press, 1993).

Obtain the video and inventory sheet titled *Identifying Your Spiritual Giftabilities* by Herb Miller, from Net Results Resource Center, 5001 Avenue N, Lubbock TX 79412-2993; phone 806/762-8094.

Resources that can aid in involving the maximum number of new members in ministry include the new-member assimilation methods described in *Every Member in Ministry* by John Ed Mathison, mentioned above, and *The Vital Congregation* by Herb Miller (Nashville: Abingdon Press). Obtain from Cokesbury: 800/672-1789 or 615/749-6113).

Chapter 9. FOLLOWING THE PAPER TRAIL

Bible Study Curriculum and Group Models

The small-group model by Roberta Hestenes is available in the audiotape package *Building Christian Community Through Small Groups.* Obtain from Fuller Theological Seminary, Media Services, Box 234, Pasadena CA 91182; phone 818/584-5227. This kit includes taped lectures, the book *Using the Bible in Small Groups,* and an expanded course syllabus.

Another helpful resource is Jeanne Hipp's book, *How to Start and Grow Small Groups in Your Church.* Obtain from Church Growth, Inc., 1921 S. Myrtle, Monrovia CA 91016; phone 800/423-4844 or 818/305-1280.

Other excellent Bible study programs: the *Disciple Bible Study* (Attn.: Wini Grizzle, Cokesbury Education Services, P.O. Box 801, Nashville TN 37202-0801—phone 800/251-8591 or

615/749-6000); *Bethel Series* (P.O. Box 8398, Madison WI 53708-8398—phone 608/849-5933); the *Kerygma Program,* particularly the introductory course titled "Discovering the Bible" (300 Mt. Lebanon Blvd., Suite 205, Pittsburgh PA 15234—phone 800/537-9462 or 412/344-6062); *Trinity Bible Studies* (Box 77, El Paso AR 72045—phone 800/848-2131 or 501-849-2131); and *Through the Bible in One Year* (Virgil W. Hensley, Inc., 6116 E. 32nd St., Tulsa OK 74135—phone 800/288-8520 or 918/664-8520).

Especially valuable with new Christians: The *Walking with God Series* by Don Cousins and Judson Poling (Grand Rapids: Zondervan Publishing House, 1992). *Leader's Guide 1* covers and includes the material in the individual booklets—*Friendship With God, The Incomparable Jesus,* and *"Follow Me!" Leader's Guide 2* covers and includes the material in the individual booklets *Discovering the Church, Building Your Church,* and *Impacting Your World.* The series is the small-group program from one of the largest churches in America, Willow Creek Community Church in South Barrington, Illinois, which has a weekend attendance of more than 15,000. Obtain from local bookstores or directly from Zondervan Publishing, 5300 Patterson Ave. S.E., Grand Rapids MI 49530; phone 800/727-3480 or 616/698-6900.

Chapter 10. THE ENCOURAGING WORD

Discussion of one chapter a month from books such as the following, which teach caring skills, will provide the necessary training for Care Team members: *Tools for Active Christians* by Herb Miller (St. Louis: CBP Press, now Chalice Press, P.O. Box 179, St. Louis MO 63166-0179—phone 800/366-3383 or 314/231-8500); and *The Caring Church* by Howard W. Stone (Minneapolis: Fortress Press, 426 S. Fifth St., Box 1209, Minneapolis MN 55440-1209—phone 800/328-4648 or 612/330-3300).

NOTES

Chapter 1. GROPING FOR THE GOOD LIFE

1. *The Good Life Catalog,* Thompson & Co., 5401 Hangar Court, P.O. Box 30303, Tampa FL 33630.
2. Janice Kastro, "Grapevine," *Time,* June 29, 1992, p. 27.
3. A. James Rudin, " 'New Age': Buyer Beware!" *The National Christian Reporter,* October 23, 1992, p. 2.
4. "TV Special Documents Revival of Spirituality," *Episcopal Life,* January 1992, p. 3.
5. *National Christian Reporter,* October 23, 1992.
6. George H. Gallup, Jr., "How It All Began," *Emerging Trends,* Summer 1992, p. 2; "PRRC Tidbits," pp. 6-7.
7. Craig Kennet Miller, *Baby Boomer Spirituality* (Nashville: Discipleship Resources, 1992), p. 34, quoting Annie Gottlieb, *Do You Believe in Magic?* (New York: Time-Life Books, 1987), p. 175.
8. "What's to Become of Secular Humanism?" *Context,* February 1, 1992, p. 4, Martin Marty quoting from and commenting on observations by Paul Kurtz in *Free Inquiry.*
9. Martin Marty, "Moses to God: Thank You for Sharing," *Context,* February 1, 1992, p. 4, quoting Leonard I. Sweet and K. Elizabeth Rennie in *Homiletic,* quoting Douglas Taylor-Weiss, rector of St. Andrew's Episcopal Church in Dayton, Ohio.
10. Jim Jones, "Did Openness Weaken the Church?" *The National Christian Reporter,* July 3, 1992, p. 1, a study of Baby Boomers raised in the Presbyterian Church (U.S.A.).
11. Gary R. Collins, *Baby Boomer Blues* (Dallas: Word, Inc., 1992), p. 193.
12. Rowland Croucher, "Spiritual Formation," *Grid* (World Vision of Australia), Winter 1991, pp. 1-2.
13. Miller, *Baby Boomer Spirituality,* p. viii.
14. George Gallup, Jr., and Timothy Jones, *The Saints Among Us* (Richfield, Conn.: Morehouse Publishing, 1992).

15. George Gallup, Jr., in a letter to Herb Miller, May 13, 1992.

16. Gallup and Jones, *The Saints Among Us*, pp. 34-87.

17. Mardelle A. Stanger, *Spiritual Formation in the Local Church* (Grand Rapids: Zondervan Publishing House, 1989), pp. 14-15.

18. Robert Stackel, "Take Your Place Among Them," *Church Management—The Clergy Journal,* January 1990, pp. 4-5.

19. Walter Shapiro, "The Birth and—Maybe—Death of Yuppies," *Time,* April 8, 1991, p. 65.

20. *Fritz Kunkel: Selected Writings,* ed. with introduction and commentary by John A. Sanford (New York: Paulist Press, 1984), p. 23.

21. Don Cousins and Judson Poling, *Friendship with God,* The Walking with God Series (Grand Rapids: Zondervan Publishing House, 1992), p. 11.

22. "Health & Science," *Time,* December 7, 1992, p. 30.

23. Louis Sullivan, "Beyond Treating Symptoms," *Urban Family,* Winter 1992, p. 6.

Chapter 2. TENDING TO BUSINESS

1. William McKinney, "Can Denominations Do Anything to Help Local Churches Grow?" workshop at the Church Growth and Decline National Research Symposium for Church and Ecumenical Leaders, Hartford Seminary, Hartford, Connecticut, April 29–May 1, 1992.

2. Wade Clark Roof, "The Baby Boom's Search for God," *American Demographics,* December 1992, pp. 50, 56.

3. C. Kirk Hadaway and David A. Roozen, "Church Growth and Decline: What Do We Know?" paper presented at the Church Growth and Decline National Research Symposium.

4. C. Kirk Hadaway, *Church Growth Principles* (Nashville: Broadman Press, 1991), p. 163.

5. Peter L. Benson and Carolyn H. Eklin, preliminary analysis from *Effective Christian Education: A National Study of Protestant Congregations—A Summary Report on Faith, Loyalty, and Congregational Life* (Search Institute, 700 Third St., Suite 210, Minneapolis, MN 55415-1138).

6. Norman Shawchuck, Philip Kotler, Bruce Wrenn, and Gustave Rath, *Marketing for Congregations* (Nashville: Abingdon Press, 1992), p. 25.

7. Mardelle A. Stanger, *Spiritual Formation in the Local Church* (Grand Rapids: Francis Asbury Press, 1989), p. 18.

8. Benson and Eklin, *Effective Christian Education.*

9. Rick Warren, "A Vision for the Whole," presented at "The Church in the 21st Century," sponsored by Leadership Network, Dallas, Texas, June 14-16, 1992.

10. George H. Gallup, Jr., and Timothy Jones, *The Saints Among Us* (Ridgefield, Conn.: Morehouse Publishing, 1992), p. 114.

11. *Emerging Trends,* Summer 1992, p.7.

12. George Barna, *The Barna Report 1992-93* (Ventura, Calif.: Regal Books, 1992), p. 41.

Chapter 3. WORSHIP IS JOB ONE

1. George Cornell, "The Public Square: A Continuing Survey of Religion and Public Life," *First Things,* P.O. Box 3000, Department FT, Denville, NJ 07834, February 1992.
2. Christopher G. Ellison, David A. Gay, and Thomas A. Glass, "Does Religious Commitment Contribute to Individual Life Satisfaction?" *Social Forces* 68:1(September 1989):100-123, reported by Norman Shawchuck, Philip Kotler, Bruce Wrenn, and Gustave Rath in *Marketing for Congregations* (Nashville: Abingdon Press, 1992), p. 65.
3. "Surface Winds or Deep Currents?" *Pulpit Helps,* January 1990, p. 14.
4. "Dull Worship Loses Blacks," *The National Christian Reporter,* July 26, 1991, p. 1.
5. *The Win Arm Growth Report,* reprinted in *Mandate,* Summer 1990, published by the General Department of Evangelism and Church Growth, the Wesleyan Church, Indianapolis, Indiana.
6. Barbara Dolan, "Full House at Willow Creek," *Time,* March 6, 1989.
7. "To Verify . . . ," *Leadership,* Summer 1992, p. 41.
8. Chuck Smith and Tal Brooke, *Harvest* (Old Tappan, N.J.: Chosen Books, 1987), pp. 15-16.
9. C. Kirk Hadaway, *Church Growth Principles* (Nashville: Broadman Press, 1991), pp. 71-72.
10. Peggy Noonan, *What I Saw at the Revolution* (New York: Random House, 1990), p. 77.

Chapter 4. JOYFUL NOISES

1. C. Kirk Hadaway, *Church Growth Principles* (Nashville: Broadman Press, 1991), p. 67.
2. "Database," *U.S. News & World Report,* February 17, 1992, p. 10.
3. George E. LaMore, Jr., "Evangelism: The World Awakening to Itself," *Forward,* Winter 1992, p. 6.
4. Hadaway, *Church Growth Principles,* p. 69.
5. Linda J. Clark, "The Music in Churches Project: The Views from the Pews," *Action Information,* July/August 1992, p. 2.
6. David R. Ray, *Small Churches Are the Right Size* (New York: Pilgrim Press, 1982), p. 71.
7. Ibid.
8. Alan Walker, *Standing Up to Preach* (Nashville: Discipleship Resources, 1983), p. 55.
9. Arthur Hailey, *The Evening News* (New York: Dell Publishing, 1990), pp. 413-14.

Chapter 5. KEEPING IN TOUCH

1. Editors of Time-Life Books, *Psychic Powers: Mysteries of the Unknown* (Alexandria, Va.: Time-Life Books, 1987), pp. 52-53.

2. *The Prison of Love,* ed. Catharine Hughes (Kansas City, Mo.: Sheed and Ward, 1972), p. 25.

3. Carl F. George, *A Consultant Looks at the 200 Barrier,* Part 2, audiotape No. 4, *Breaking the 200 Barrier: New Model for Leadership* (Pasadena, Calif.: Fuller Evangelistic Association, 1982).

4. Herb Miller, *The Secret to Abundant Living: Learning How to Ask* (Lubbock, Tex.: Net Press, 1988, 1992).

5. Pastor's column, church newsletter, Melonie Park Baptist Church, Lubbock, Texas, March-April 1988.

6. Alvin J. Vander Griend, "How to Develop a Praying Church," *Net Results,* January 1991, p. 15.

7. George Gallup, Jr., and George O'Connell, *Who Do Americans Say I Am?* (Philadelphia: Westminster Press, 1986), p. 89.

8. George Dolan, "This Is West Texas," *Fort Worth Star Telegram,* August 25, 1969.

9. Vander Griend, "How to Develop a Praying Church," p. 15.

10. Rob Portlock, *Climbing the Church Walls* (Downers Grove, Ill.: Intervarsity Press, 1991).

Chapter 6. THE PEOPLE CONNECTION

1. Larry Keefauver, former National Events Director for *Group Magazine,* in a sermon at First Christian Church (Disciples of Christ), Lubbock, Texas.

2. George H. Gallup, Jr., and Timothy Jones, *The Saints Among Us* (Ridgefield, Conn.: Morehouse Publishing, 1992), p. 100.

3. George Barna, *Finding a Church You Can Call Home* (Ventura, Calif.: Regal Books, 1992), p. 93.

4. Gallup and Jones, *Saints Among Us,* p. 94.

5. Bruce Larson, in a letter to Herb Miller, May 7, 1992.

6. Princeton Religion Research Center, "Mega Churches or Small Groups?" *Emerging Trends,* October 1991, pp. 1, 6.

7. Cynthia B. Astle, "Most Churches Don't Cultivate Saints," *The National Christian Reporter,* July 10, 1992, p. 1.

8. Gregg Childress and Stephen D. Bryant, "Up and Running with 'The Walk to Emmaus,'" *Net Results,* September 1991, p. 12.

Chapter 7. TURNING ON THE LIGHTS

1. George A. Miller, "Giving Away Psychology in the 80's," *Psychology Today,* January 1980, p. 41.

2. "Preaching Through the Year," *The Clergy Journal,* May/June 1989, p. 60.

3. Hannah Whitall Smith, quoting Coleridge in *The God of All Comfort* (New York: Ballantine Books, 1986), p. 85.

4. Bert Decker, "How to Use the Visual Factor When Presenting and Speaking," *Communication Briefings*, p. 8a, quoting a study by Albert Mehrabian at UCLA.

5. Mal King, "Downwind from the Pulpit," *Pulpit & Bible Study Helps*, March 1992, p. 2.

6. *Pulpit Helps*, March 1980.

Chapter 8. ON THE SERVING LINES

1. Leighton Ford, "What Can Fill an Empty Frame?" address at Congress 88, Chicago, August 4–7, 1988.

2. Robert W. Wuthnow, Virginia A. Hodgkinson & Associates, *Faith and Philanthropy in America* (San Francisco: Jossey-Bass, 1990), pp. 9-10.

3. Archibald MacLeish, *Time*, December 22, 1958.

4. Gerald Kennedy, *Have This Mind* (New York: Harper & Brothers, 1948), pp. 94-95.

5. Manis Friedman, *Doesn't Anyone Blush Anymore?* (San Francisco: HarperCollins, 1990), pp. 32-33.

6. *The Executive Speech Writer Newsletter*, 1989, Vol. 4, p. 8.

7. Grayson L. Tucker, "Enhancing Church Vitality Through Congregational Identity Change," *The Mainstream Protestant "Decline,"* ed. Milton J. Coalter, John M. Mulder, and Louis B. Weeks (Louisville, Ky.: Westminster/John Knox Press), p. 73.

Chapter 9. FOLLOWING THE PAPER TRAIL

1. "Eating the Bible," *Pulpit Helps*, August 1991, p. 27.

2. *Pulpit Helps*, September 1980.

3. Lance Morrow, "When the Earth Cracks Open," *Time*, October 30, 1989, p. 100.

4. Michael J. Hostetler, *Illustrating the Sermon* (Grand Rapids: Zondervan Publishing House, 1989), p. 49.

Chapter 10. THE ENCOURAGING WORD

1. Mike Schafer, "To Illustrate . . . ," *Leadership*, Summer 1992, p. 46, quoting Charles Swindoll, *Stress Fractures*.

2. *Sales & Marketing Management*, October 1992, quoted in *Media Management Newsletter*, December 1992, p. 2.

3. Ronald A. Wanless, "Listening Actively," *Net Results*, May 1990, pp. 1-3.

4. Richard Ostling, "Handmaid or Feminist?" *Time*, December 30, 1991, pp. 62-63, quoted in "Mary: Handmaid or Feminist?" *Current Thoughts and Trends*, February 1992, p. 5.

5. W. James Cowell, *Extending Your Congregations's Welcome* (Nashville: Discipleship Resources, 1989), pp. 44-45.